Government and Science

GOVERNMENT AND SCIENCE

Their Dynamic Relation
in American Democracy

DON K. PRICE

A Galaxy Book

OXFORD UNIVERSITY PRESS
New York 1962

PREFACE

The immediate reason I undertook to write this book was an invitation from New York University to deliver the 1953 James Stokes Lectures on Politics.

The deeper reason was a notion that had been developing in my mind for several years (not a particularly original one) that the development of public policy and of the methods of its administration owed less in the long run to the processes of conflict among political parties and social or economic pressure groups than to the more objective processes of research and discussion among professional groups.

While working with the Public Administration Clearing House in Chicago, in association with the dozen or more organizations of public officials that have their headquarters at 1313 East Sixtieth Street, I was struck by the way in which a professional consensus, based on the findings of research of a scientific or semiscientific nature, often brought about the adoption of a new public policy and determined the method of its administration. This does not mean that I concluded that this process did not need to be under democratic control; on the contrary, it began to seem to me that it could operate only under democratic control, and that effective democratic control depended on an underpinning of this kind of professional and scientific activity.

My interest in the subject was intensified while serving in the United States Coast Guard, which now administers several of the programs that in the early nineteenth century were founded by the organized efforts of scientists—especially the steamboat inspection service and the lighthouse service, which were among the first federal efforts to regulate private commerce and to provide it with essential services. My interest was further developed when I worked in the Bureau of the Budget on the legislation that created the Atomic Energy Commission and the National Science Foundation. And it continued during several years of association with the Research and Development Board of the Department of Defense, first as a part-time consultant and as chairman of the Board's Security Review Committee, and later, during 1952 and 1953, as the Board's Deputy Chairman.

In this series of jobs I began to be aware that the activities of scientists, which had always been unusually influential in the public policies of the United States, were becoming responsible for significant changes in the nature of the American governmental system. The subject seemed to me to cry out for attention and to involve a whole series of most profound and most neglected problems. All that this series of essays can do is to ask a few of the questions, and to express the hope that other students can go far more deeply into their history and their theory, while others in the public service can begin to answer them in practice.

This book could never have been written if Public Administration Clearing House, to which I returned in May 1953 from the Department of Defense, had not permitted me to devote a large part of the summer of 1953 to the preparation of the first draft, which was completed before I joined the staff of the Ford Foundation in October. For this, and even more for his personal encouragement and advice, I am deeply indebted to Herbert Emmerich, Director of Public Administration Clearing House.

In the planning and original preparation of this material I trespassed for many hours on the time and patience of the former Director of Public Administration Clearing House, Louis Brownlow, whose wisdom and historical insight have been the most important influence in my education. I also had the invaluable advice at this stage of S. Douglas Cornell, Executive Director of the National Academy of Science and the National Research Council, who has had a rare opportunity to observe the new methods by which science and public policy are interwoven.

I am indebted to several others for having given a great deal of time and thought to reading and criticizing the preliminary draft of my manuscript.

Vannevar Bush, President of the Carnegie Institution of Washington, read most of the preliminary draft and helped me greatly by his vigorous and pointed criticism. No one else has had so much to do in recent years with guiding the developments that this book seeks to describe. I have ventured to disagree with Dr. Bush on several points, but I am none the less grateful for his generous advice.

Pendleton Herring, President of the Social Science Research Council, was kind enough to invite me to discuss the general argument of this book, and particularly of its sixth chapter, at the annual meeting of the Council's Board of Directors in September 1953. Council meetings have been the scene of lively arguments in this general field ever since it was explored from 1945 to 1947 by the Council's Committee on Federal Government and Research, and I have profited greatly by these discussions.

I am most grateful for the help of several friends who read all or major parts of the manuscript and gave me the benefit of their advice, but who should not be held responsible for any of the errors of fact and opinion that remain in the book.

Among them are James A. Perkins, Vice President of the Carnegie Corporation of New York; E. R. Piore, Chief Scientist of the Office of Naval Research; Alan Waterman, Director of the National Science Foundation, and C. E. Sunderlin, its Deputy Director; and several of those with whom I had the privilege of working at the Research and Development Board —in particular the former Chairman of the Board, Walter G. Whitman, now of the Department of Chemical Engineering at the Massachusetts Institute of Technology, and Mrs. Astrid Kraus, Charles M. Mottley, and F. J. Sette.

DON K. PRICE

Alexandria, Virginia
December 1953

CONTENTS

I

THE REPUBLICAN REVOLUTION
page 1

II

FREEDOM OR RESPONSIBILITY?
page 32

III

FEDERALISM BY CONTRACT
page 65

IV

SECURITY AND PUBLICITY RISKS
page 95

V

THE MACHINERY OF ADVICE
page 124

VI

THE STRUCTURE OF POLICY
page 160

VII

NEW WINE IN NEW BOTTLES
page 190

Government and Science

I

THE
REPUBLICAN REVOLUTION

At the end of World War II the mood of the scientific community was in sharp contrast to that of the general public. The popular magazines were full of advertisements promising that the great advances of science during the war would lead to a postwar utopia of new gadgets. But the scientists themselves were generally not so cheerful; indeed, their very success as scientists had made them fearful or pessimistic as citizens. To them—or to some of the more far-sighted among them—the invention of the atomic bomb was a threat to the freedom of the world, and particularly to the freedom of science.

These fears have by now become more widely accepted. The United States has come to see that it is in a new kind of rivalry with the Soviet Union—a rivalry that may well turn, not on territorial or diplomatic gains, or even (in the narrow sense of the word) on military advantage. The crucial advantage in the issue of power is likely to be with the nation whose scientific program can produce the next revolutionary advance in military tactics, following those already made by radar, jet propulsion, and nuclear fission.

Partially obscured by this spectacular military aspect of the role of science, but closely related to it, is its long-range economic aspect. The same fields of technology that are crucial to military tactics—electronic communications, aeronautics, and power—are also those that may have great influence in economic competition. The massing of scientific research for attack on military problems has its industrial by-products. In these fields the tremendous military research program is probably pushing our industry farther and farther ahead of its competitors, at a time when the most difficult economic problems of the free world arise because we can produce more things more cheaply than can our allies.

American science in its relation to government is in an uncomfortable pair of dilemmas. The main article of its faith is academic freedom, which would clearly be extinguished by a Communist triumph. To prevent such a triumph, American scientists are now required to work in a complicated network of secret and confidential data, and to communicate on many subjects only with those who have been officially investigated and cleared. Then, too, science has been accustomed in the past to rely for its support (and incidentally for its independence) on a great variety of local and private institutions. Yet it is now obvious to everyone that the structure of scientific research in American universities and industry has come to depend heavily on federal grants and federal contracts.

It is not surprising that many scientists have come to look on this relationship between science and government as an unhappy shotgun marriage, into which science had been frightened by the explosive force that it now measures in millions (instead of merely in thousands) of tons of TNT. They take this view even when they realize that they have helped to create a world in which the United States cannot be defended except by the maximum development of science, and in which science cannot be protected in its freedom, or supported with funds, except by government.

A very small minority of scientists in America have followed some of their European colleagues in looking to government as the savior of science from the capitalist system. Many more have tended to look on government as an authoritative and arbitrary institution controlled by politicians or bureaucrats who have little sympathy for the advancement of knowledge or the interests of private institutions.

Neither attitude seems to me to have much to do with the way that American government actually works today. Those who react automatically in favor of business as against government, or vice versa, or for civilian as against military institutions, or for private as against public institutions, are likely to find themselves in strangely contradictory positions. By classical textbook standards the American system of government is a maze of paradoxes—a confusing conglomeration in which private institutions have a major role in the planning of government policy, in which scientific advisers are held publicly responsible for some of the most critical decisions of war planning and the ivory tower of anonymity is reserved for generals and admirals, and in which Congressional committees check on administrative details while policy is developed either by trade associations or by harassed government clerks.

Yet this system, to the wonder of the foreigner—and, even more, of the informed insider—seems to work with a surprisingly dynamic quality. It is dynamic, it seems to me, because science, which has been the most explosive force in modern society, has profoundly influenced the development of the American government ever since the scientists took a hand in the great republican revolution of the eighteenth century. Unless we look at the way in which science helped first to shatter the authority of sovereigns, and then helped to rebuild authority in quite different patterns, we cannot understand the new relationship of science to government of the mid-twentieth century.

In looking at this new relationship, I shall not try to distinguish very carefully between basic and applied science, or to decide whether social science is really science at all. For I am interested in the influence on our governmental institutions, not of any particular scientific method, but of an attitude that scientists of all descriptions have shared, by contrast with politicians, clergymen, and lawyers. The scientist does not appeal to precedent or take things on faith. He wants to observe them, experiment with them, and prove them. This attitude, moreover, has spread during the past century or two among the general public. Though it began with the scientists, it then spread to the allied professions and the "mechanic arts," so that it is impossible to talk about the political consequences of science and refer only to the influence of scientists. It is the modern factual and objective way of thinking, which the scientist stimulated, that has worked on our political system indirectly, by way of the general climate of informed opinion.

We may as well start at the beginning, constitutionally speaking. The American Revolution and the American Constitution were the first great practical steps toward destroying the traditional conception of sovereignty and the traditional apparatus of hereditary rule. In Europe it was the age of the Enlightenment and the Encyclopedists—the rationalists who found themselves at odds with the existing apparatus of society. But in Europe there were no practical statesmen on the order of those who shaped the changes that revolutionized America well ahead of France. Washington, the surveyor and engineer who kept up a correspondence with Arthur Young on methods of scientific agriculture; Franklin, the inventor and experimenter; and Jefferson, who took an active personal lead in stimulating a wide range of scientific studies from paleontology to meteorology—these were the men who set the intellectual tone among the leaders in the American colonies.

The first effect of their leadership was to destroy the traditional theory of hereditary sovereignty, and to substitute the idea that the people had the right, by rational and experimental processes, to build their governmental institutions to suit themselves. The new government could not rest on a basis of either dynastic authority or military force. Its basis had to be a representative republican system. That system had to depend on elections, in constituencies that did not exist by virtue of grants from the king. The people, in short, had to be the basis of political power. Accordingly, the people had to be counted, and for the first time in modern history a nation instituted a complete census.

The census thus became the ultimate basis of sovereign power in the United States. The Constitution itself required the federal government to make the largest collection of social-science data in the world, and the census is still the most important source of materials for social-science research. There are those who believe that the government cannot properly support research in the social sciences because of their controversial nature. Yet today the most significant redistribution of political power in America is accomplished by the clerks in the Bureau of the Census, who each ten years calculate the new representation of the states in the House of Representatives. Even though the decennial census has been one of the great occasions for the distribution of political patronage, hardly anyone has questioned the integrity of the Census Bureau's basic information.

The American Revolution was so thorough—partly, of course, because it took place in a relatively new country and partly because the leading Tories were forced to emigrate—that the fundamental issues in American society developed during the next two centuries in an almost unique form. The French liberals had to spend the nineteenth century fighting the entrenched military and ecclesiastical establishments, which still exercised profound influence within the permanent institutions of government. In Great Britain the liberals were similarly engaged in restricting the royal prerogative and destroying the remnants of feudal privilege. Meanwhile, in Great Britain as well as on the Continent, the old ruling class assimilated the new captains of industry.

It was therefore very easy for the European liberal to accept Marx's view that the government was a great permanent engine for the defense of the privileged capitalist classes, and thus the more liberal wing in politics moved fairly steadily toward various forms of socialism as a solution to its problems.

In America this trend did not make much sense to anyone. The government was not permanent enough, or efficient enough, to be thought of as an engine for anything. In early America it was, indeed, the conservatives who sought to make the government an instrument of national economic and industrial planning, and it was the triumphant democracy that destroyed their dream. The intellectual center of this dream was the idea of a national university—a center for the advancement of the sciences recommended by President Washington and by several of his successors. Alexander Hamilton made the keystone of his system for the development of American manufactures a system of government bounties and subsidies to scientists and inventors, to accompany the use of tariffs and other government policies for the encouragement of industrialization.[1] John Quincy Adams followed George Washington in believing that the key to the preservation of the Union was the use of all the resources of the applied sciences to create a system of transportation and communications to develop the West and to link together the North and the South.

As John Quincy Adams wrote in a personal letter in 1837:

[1] "Report on Manufactures" in *The Works of Alexander Hamilton* (New York: Williams and Whiting, 1810), Vol. I, pp. 235-36.

The great effort of my administration was to mature into a permanent and regular system the application of all the superfluous revenue of the Union to internal improvement. . . . With this system in ten years from this day the surface of the whole Union would have been checkered over with railroads and canals. It may still be done half a century later and with the limping gait of State legislature and private adventure. I would have done it in the administration of the affairs of the nation.[2]

John Quincy Adams was the last of the great statesmen of the Federalist period who united with politics a deep personal interest in science. As Secretary of State he personally prepared for the Congress a *Report upon Weights and Measures;*[3] as an elder statesman in Congress he continued to fight for a wide variety of scientific programs; and he finally killed himself by traveling at an advanced age in bad weather to Cincinnati to dedicate an astronomical observatory.

His grandson, Brooks Adams, has called attention to his fundamental belief:

He alone among public men of that period appreciated that a nation to flourish under conditions of modern economic competition, must organize its administrative, as well as its social system upon scientific principles.

But this was a futile dream. John Quincy Adams had inherited from the Federalists and the Jeffersonians alike the ideal of a competent public service. But, to quote Brooks Adams again:

[2] To the Reverend Charles W. Upham. Quoted in Henry Adams, *The Degradation of the Democratic Dogma* (with an introduction by Brooks Adams) (New York: The Macmillan Company, 1919), pp. 24-25.

[3] John Quincy Adams, Secretary of State of the United States, *Report Upon Weights and Measures, prepared in obedience to a resolution of the Senate of the Third March, 1817* (Washington: Gales and Seaton, 1821). Thomas Jefferson, as Secretary of State, had submitted to the House of Representatives on July 17, 1790, a *Report of the Secretary of State on the Subject of Establishing the Uniformity of the Weights, Measures, and Coins of the United States.*

Government and Science

As John Quincy Adams discovered in 1828, democracy would not permit the ablest staff of officials, to be chosen by him, to administer the public trust. Democracy, on the contrary, has insisted on degrading the public service to a common level of incapacity, thereby throwing the management of all difficult public problems, such as the use of railroads and canals, into private hands, in order that they might escape ruin, and thence has come the predicament in which we, in particular, and the world at large, now stand.[4]

This was a revolution even more drastic in some of its practical effects than that of 1776. The earlier revolution denied the old theory of sovereignty; the later one made government ineffective as a working organization. In this respect the states and cities outdid the federal government. As they adopted new constitutions and charters they not only made their personnel systems subject to political spoils, but also made their forms of organization diffuse and emasculated their powers.

This system might have worked indefinitely if America had remained the frontier as Andrew Jackson knew it, or had developed according to the agrarian ideals of Jefferson. But just as the philosophical scientists of the eighteenth century had begun the process of weakening the authority of government, so the applied scientists of the nineteenth century—the engineers and inventors—made necessary the strengthening of its structure and authority. They built up the modern corporation, the modern metropolitan area, and the great concentrations of economic power and social problems that could not be dealt with by the weak governments of the frontier. For this development the American people were intellectually quite unprepared. They had neither the legal theory nor the estab-

---

4 Introduction by Brooks Adams in Henry Adams, *The Degradation of the Democratic Dogma* (New York: The Macmillan Company, 1919), pp. 61, 120-21.

lished administrative machinery to cope with problems that could be solved only by the steady policies of a strong government.

Science took part in the republican revolution that destroyed the old system of sovereign authority. It was then forced, by the very changes that it effected in society, to take part in the rebuilding of the machinery of government. Constitutional historians have always noted how the radicalism of the Declaration of Independence had to be counterbalanced by the conservatism of the Constitution. But they have less often observed that the pervasive weakening of authority and administration that went with the republican revolution continued for nearly a century. And then science had a hand in developing the legal theory and the administrative machinery that were needed to make the federal Constitution—and the state constitutions and municipal charters—workable in modern society.

Science did so, first of all, by helping to show that government needed to add to its legal powers to deal with modern problems. It became clear that life in industrial cities would be intolerable without more regulation by government than was possible under a Jeffersonian political theory. It is hard in the mid-twentieth century to appreciate how much the city dweller depends for his health and safety on governmental controls that were legally impossible a century ago—on public health regulations, on city planning and zoning, and on fire, electrical, and building inspection, to say nothing of the positive municipal services. At the same time the farmer has gone even farther than the city dweller in requiring the government to sustain and regulate his aspect of the national economy.

The powers for these purposes were added to government only gradually, and only because the law began to find that there were issues that could not be settled entirely by legal precedent or by reasoning from abstract principles. It began

9

to take note of proof furnished by the sciences and of the informed opinion of organized professional groups.

It is important to note that in all this process the initiative and leadership came from local scientific and professional groups or from local groups of laymen interested in science. Their interest was usually based not on the cultivation of science for its own sake, but on the solution of practical problems. But in the end it led the government not only to undertake scientific research, but also to expand its powers, its functions, and its personnel to take advantage of the new opportunities developed by research and experimentation.

Let us have a look first at the way some of the regulatory powers of government developed. Throughout the nineteenth century judges were gradually persuaded that public health regulations were necessary for the prevention of epidemics. These regulations were extended from the simple provisions of quarantine to a wide variety of sanitary regulations, and finally to the provision of authority for zoning and city planning in the interests of the public health and safety. Gradually the massing of medical evidence regarding contagious disease, and the relation of such evidence to the sociological statistics regarding urban life in general, provided the basis for the development of municipal powers in America.

The federal government, making use of its constitutional power to control commerce, began to extend its regulatory functions as soon as the local governments themselves. Alexander Dallas Bache, the great-grandson of Benjamin Franklin, was the professor of natural philosophy and chemistry at the University of Pennsylvania. Professor Bache became chairman of a special committee at the Franklin Institute in 1832 to investigate the reasons for the explosions of steamboat boilers. The Secretary of the Treasury, with the help of a special appropriation of the Congress, contributed $1,500 toward the expenses of this investigation—probably the first grant by the federal government for experimental research.

The committee reported in 1836 with a magnificent disregard for the limitations of science. It first discussed such scientific problems as the manifestations of steam pressure and the qualities of various types of iron and copper boilers, but then went on to recommend to the Congress a draft bill providing for the first program of federal regulation of business. The bill was enacted, and the Steamboat Inspection Service became the first federal regulatory agency.[5]

Progress in the physical and biological sciences, medicine, and engineering made perhaps the first important contribution to the development of government powers and programs, but the social sciences were not far behind. The regulation of business by both the federal and state governments began to develop in the late nineteenth century. This development would hardly have been possible without the economic and statistical studies that began to expand at that time. J. D. B. De Bow, who headed the Census Bureau when it conducted the census of 1850—containing some statistical series even more elaborate than those of today—founded *De Bow's Review*, the first economics journal in America, and gave great impetus to the development of this whole field of study. Not much later the studies of John R. Commons laid the groundwork for the twentieth-century advances in labor legislation, and the research of Charles Francis Adams on problems of transportation economics led directly to the regulation of the railroads, first by the states, and then by the federal government through the Interstate Commerce Commission. As for the rail-

---

[5] Committee of the Franklin Institute of the State of Pennsylvania for the Promotion of the Mechanic Arts, *General Report on the Explosions of Steam-Boilers* (Philadelphia: C. Sherman & Co. Printers, 19 St. James Street, 1836).

roads, of course, the social and natural sciences joined hands in encouraging federal regulation; the Franklin Institute, appalled by the railway wrecks as it had been earlier by the steamboat disasters, worked out a uniform code of railway signals, which was enacted into federal legislation.[6]

The history textbooks are accustomed to trace the development of governmental policy in relation to party campaigns and changes in national administration. as they are likely to credit the revolution in technology to the inventions of an Edison, Morse, or Bell. But just as these inventors were simply carrying to conclusion the work of scientists still comparatively unknown to the public, so the development of government powers and functions during the past century has been only the inevitable adoption by politicians of ideas first developed in scientific laboratories and in scholarly or professional societies.

But this is getting ahead of our story. Let us look for a moment at the way in which the government began to support science during the nineteenth century.

First of all there is the story of the agricultural sciences. In this field government support was no novelty, even at the time when President Washington first proposed to the Congress the establishment of a National Board of Agriculture. Parliament under the Puritan Commonwealth had granted funds for experimentation in Georgia on the growth of indigo and other agricultural products.

The creation of a federal agricultural agency, like the rest of the grand design of the Federalists for the development of the national economy, was blocked by Jefferson's strict construction of the Constitution. Nevertheless, Jefferson as an individual gave a great impetus to the support of the agricultural sciences. In 1787, for example, he smuggled rice out

---

[6] Thomas Coulson, "The First Hundred Years of Research at the Franklin Institute," *Journal of the Franklin Institute*, CCLVI, No. 1 (July 1953).

of Piedmont in spite of the laws prohibiting its export on pain of death, and encouraged the founding of agricultural societies and their co-operation on a national basis.

In the development of a new continent the great opportunity of the applied sciences was in the mapping of the country, the surveying of its natural resources, and the improvement of its agriculture. On the recommendation of the American Philosophical Society President Jefferson transmitted to the Congress a proposal for the establishment of the United States Coast Survey, which was set up in the Treasury Department in 1807. The American Association for the Advancement of Science was created when the American Society of Geologists and Naturalists decided to broaden its scope and change its name. Expeditions like those of Lewis and Clark, whom President Jefferson sent out to explore the West, were only spectacular extensions of the work being carried on in a great many states. The first President of the A.A.A.S. had been a state geologist in Massachusetts, New York, and Vermont,[7] and the agricultural experiment stations in the states, which began without federal support, grew out of the work of the geological surveys.

About this time began the active co-operation of the private agricultural societies with government officials. This was a reciprocal business. Public officials encouraged and stimulated the growth of the private organizations. The Commissioner of Patents in the State Department, who had begun as early as 1836 to distribute free seeds to farmers, helped organize the Agricultural Society of the United States; and after the Civil War officials in the new Department of Agriculture helped organize the National Grange. But the pressure was far more continuous and effective in the opposite direction. The national official agencies were created by the initiative and support of

---

[7] Frederick W. True, *A History of the First Half-Century of the National Academy of Sciences, 1863-1913* (Washington; National Academy of Sciences, 1913), p. 152.

the private associations. The New York State Agricultural Society from 1832, and the United States Agricultural Society from 1852, worked steadily for the creation of state experiment stations and for the creation of a national Department of Agriculture.[8]

The support of the agricultural sciences—into which the greater part of the federal research funds went until World War II—was based not only on the recommendations of local groups of scientists, but also on the more widespread demand from the farmers and their organizations. The seeds that Jefferson smuggled out of Europe and those that American consuls sent back for experimental purposes in later years led Congressmen to the habit of sending out free seeds to their constituents —an important item of patronage for more than a century and one that helped educate Congress to the need for technical assistance to American farmers.

It was such practical politics that shaped the system of federal aid to agricultural research. In 1862 Congress might have decided to give funds for agricultural research to the principal existing universities, where the best research could have been had for the money. It might have given funds to the Smithsonian Institution or set up laboratories directly in some federal agency.

Instead the Congress, in the same year that it created the Department of Agriculture, passed the Morrill Act and the Homestead Act. These two acts followed the precedent of the grant of federal lands for education in the Northwest Territory in 1787—grants of free land for what amounted to relief purposes and for bonuses to veterans of the Revolution. The Homestead Act followed the appeal of the Republican Party

---

8 A. C. True, *A History of Agricultural Experimentation and Research in the United States, 1607-1925* (Washington: Government Printing Office, 1937), Misc. Pub. No. 251, United States Department of Agriculture.

to "vote yourself a farm," and the Morrill Act set up a system of grants of public lands to the states to support the creation of colleges—the land-grant colleges—for training in the agricultural and mechanic arts. By the end of the century the land-grant system had been expanded into a system of cash grants to the states for the support of experiment stations associated with the A. and M. colleges.

This policy was doubtless not the most efficient and economical way to produce first-rate basic research. It led to the support of a great many institutions that the better established universities condescendingly called the "cow colleges." It led to a great deal of research in which the practical problems of the local farmers were considered far more important than basic scientific principles. But it did cover the country with institutions for training and research in the agricultural sciences and engineering, a system that has no parallel in any other country.

Since this system owed its beginning to political pressure, it is not surprising that the distribution of grants for agricultural research was not accompanied, in the early days, by any very effective central supervision. The funds were divided among the experiment stations according to a statutory formula rather than by administrative discretion. And it was many years before the development of the research bureaus in the Department of Agriculture, and the threat of such pests as the boll weevil, gave the Department of Agriculture a role of effective leadership over the state experiment stations.

By beginning with scientific experimentation and later moving on into research in agricultural economics, the Department of Agriculture laid the foundations of the whole range of federal programs for the encouragement, support, and control of agriculture on a national basis—a system that has made the supposedly most individualistic class in American society the enthusiastic supporters of a thoroughgoing national system of technical aid and economic regulation. In no field is there a clearer line of connection between the development of scientific research and the subsequent development of governmental authority and programs.

In other fields of science the relationship with government developed in different patterns. During the nineteenth century, two institutions deserve particular attention: the Smithsonian Institution and the National Academy of Sciences. Whereas the system of agricultural research grew up gradually, and its shape was determined by political considerations, these two institutions were created by scientists and conformed to their ideas about the proper relationship of government and science.

The Smithsonian Institution was not incorporated until 1846, but it was the fruit of the ideas of a half century earlier. James Smithson, the illegitimate son of the Duke of Northumberland, was (like Priestley) one of the English scientists who were sympathetic to the ideas of the American and French revolutions. In 1792 he was in Paris, singing *Ça Ira* and writing home letters that were unmistakably republican in sentiment. In later years he continued to live abroad, perhaps disillusioned with politics and certainly resentful of the fact that his illegitimacy barred him from the social station of his ancestors in English society. He doubtless believed that the radical and rational young republic of Franklin and Jefferson was better able than England to use his estate, as he said in his will, for "the increase and diffusion of knowledge among men."

Smithson died in 1829, the year in which Andrew Jackson became President. By the time his bequest reached the United States, democracy was no longer a theory in the United States—it was a fact that had all the imperfections of most political facts. The scientists and their sponsors in the Congress—par-

ticularly John Quincy Adams, who led the fight for the accept-
ance of Smithson's bequest—were no longer in the vanguard
of revolutionary politics. On the contrary, they were eager to
establish the Smithsonian Institution under a form of organization that would insulate it as far as possible from partisan
politics and protect its privately donated capital from political
abuse.

Ironically enough, the original capital was invested in bonds
of the state of Arkansas, which defaulted on them, but the
federal government restored the full amount and guaranteed
the Smithsonian six per cent interest perpetually. Nevertheless,
and although the Institution is listed as a part of the organization of the federal government, it has always liked to consider
itself a private trust rather than a government agency.[9]

As far as I know, the only function ever vested by law in
the President's Cabinet is that of serving as the membership
of the Smithsonian Establishment. But the Establishment,
though composed of the principal heads of the executive departments, has nothing to do with running the Institution.
That is the responsibility of the Board of Regents; this executive board is made up mainly of officials from the judicial and
legislative branches of the government and filled out by the
appointment of several private citizens. It in turn delegates its
executive function to the Secretary whom it appoints.

The Smithsonian defies classification, but it may well be
thought of as the first American foundation of national scope.
It had many of the qualities of the later private foundations,
for it pioneered in a great many fields and left the further
development of its ideas to other institutions. One of the seven

---

9 The Institution proper is supported by the income of its endowments, which
have grown as a result of private gifts to many times the original sum given
by Smithson. The Secretary of the Smithsonian, however, administers the
United States National Museum and nine other smaller federal agencies that
are wholly supported by annual appropriations made by the Congress.

secretaries who have served it since 1836 helped found the National Academy of Sciences; another originated the Marine Biological Station at Woods Hole, Massachusetts; and another took the lead in establishing the Carnegie Institution of Washington and in organizing the National Advisory Committee for Aeronautics. The Institution was a tremendous influence in developing the scientific activities of a dozen or more federal agencies during the nineteenth century. Its more recent history, however, suggests that there are handicaps as well as advantages in the form of government organization that is divorced from political control and from operating programs. The newer and more exciting functions have gone to other agencies, while the Smithsonian has been loaded down with the administrative burdens of a group of museums and a zoo, which take up about nine tenths of its budget.

The National Academy of Sciences was not a new idea when it was chartered by the Congress in 1863. The Civil War simply gave the scientists a chance to establish an institution of which they had been dreaming for decades. The same men who had advocated a national university during the Federalist period had discussed the creation of a National Academy; indeed, the two ideas were sometimes indistinguishable.

By 1851 Professor Bache, in a speech as President of the A.A.A.S., had proposed the creation of a National Academy to provide scientific advice to government agencies. "There are few applications of Science," he argued, "which do not bear on the interests of commerce and navigation, naval or military concerns, the customs, the light-houses, the public lands, post-offices and post-roads, either directly or remotely."

To give the government help on such problems was one purpose of the Academy; another was to supply a kind of honorific distinction that had been missing in American intellectual life. Joseph Henry, as President of the Academy in

1867, referred wistfully to the honors and rewards given scientists by the academies of Paris, Berlin, and St. Petersburg and hoped that the Academy would supply similar incentives to encourage "devotion to original research," as contrasted with mechanical inventions. At the same time, to justify the complete detachment of the Academy from government control, its charter sought to protect it, as its first President noted, from suspicion of any "taint of self-seeking as to power or influence," or "taint of supposed desire for remuneration,"[10] by simply providing that it could never be paid for its work for the government beyond the actual expense of its investigations.

The organization of the Academy was more suited to the purpose of providing honor to its members than advice to the government. It was a self-perpetuating group, limited at first to fifty members, which had to set up an *ad hoc* committee to consider each request for help from an official agency. Yet the work of the Academy was fruitful not only in furthering science, but in its effects on the operating programs of government.

For example, the scientists were the first to recognize that America was destroying its natural resources by wasteful methods of development. The A.A.A.S. had lobbied for years in favor of federal laws to protect the remaining forests. Perhaps the most crucial step toward a new federal policy, however, was the creation in 1896 of the National Academy's Committee on the Inauguration of a National Forest Policy. The report of this committee, of which Gifford Pinchot was a member, led to the creation of the United States Forest Service, and Pinchot later credited it with originating the federal forest policy.[11]

[10] Frederick W. True, *A History of the First Half-Century of the National Academy of Sciences, 1863-1913* (Washington: National Academy of Sciences, 1913) , p. 203.

[11] *Yearbook of the United States Department of Agriculture, 1899* (Washington: Government Printing Office, 1900) , p. 297. This Yearbook, as its Preface

Similarly, it was as a result of committee reports from the National Academy that the Congress set up the Geological Survey to unify and develop the survey work of the Department of the Interior and created the Weather Bureau as a civilian agency to carry on the work originally done by the Army Signal Corps.

We have already seen how the work of the agricultural experiment stations led to the present broad programs of the Department of Agriculture, and we have noted the geological and other survey work that led to the programs of the Forest Service and of the Department of Interior. A little later the Department of Commerce and Labor was established, primarily to carry on research on industrial and labor problems. These research programs included that of the National Bureau of Standards, for which the National Academy had lobbied for some time. But they also included a wide range of social-science research. These research programs gradually broadened to form the basis of the subsequent programs of Commerce and Labor when they were set up as separate departments, and of the emergency programs of public assistance and wartime regulation of the economy. Thus the research programs of natural and social scientists laid the foundation for the development of government services, the extension of governmental powers, and the regulation of key aspects of the national economy.

The federal government, after starting with a theory that denied the traditional doctrines of sovereignty, gradually built up its powers and functions to make use of the applied sciences for the development of the new continent, and ultimately to meet the needs of an industrialized economy. In this process

says, presented "for the first time within the covers of a single volume a fairly comprehensive review of the progress and development of a century in almost every branch of scientific inquiry having a direct practical bearing upon agriculture."

the national associations and organizations of scientists and their professional colleagues—working within their specialized groups without regard to partisan allegiance or to the boundaries between government and private life—supplied the most dynamic initiative.

But the same scientists who led the government to undertake its new functions were far from willing to build up the government as an authoritative central power. The public agencies that they helped to create were often so organized as to make them as independent of the heads of government as if they were private institutions. Americans learned early that it was possible, especially in the states and municipalities, to create public agencies that were a part of the general government in name and financial support only. In this respect the scientists were often in alliance with the lawyers, who were eager to leave as little discretionary power as possible in the hands of those who administered the laws. So the habit developed of delegating new functions to independent boards or commissions, which were supposed to operate on the basis of scientific or professional judgment and with as little mixture of politics as possible.

These boards were usually staffed by government personnel and supported by public funds. Yet many of them, with the moral and political support of their professional colleagues and clients, maintained for many years a high degree of independence of the mayor or governor or legislature. They were usually not very efficient and are now going out of fashion—except, of course, in the field of education—but they may have been necessary for the creation of professional respectability and *esprit de corps* as the government undertook new functions.

In the federal government the Constitution made it more difficult to set up such independent boards, somewhat to the distress of the National Academy, which repeatedly recommended that boards of scientists be created to head research and related programs. This was all to the good, from the administrator's point of view. But a sound constitutional structure was not, by itself, enough to provide good administration. It could not provide an adequate career service or create competent executives. John Quincy Adams, for all his administrative ability as Secretary of State, saw the Patent Office fall into chaos because its head was a scientist more interested in organizing subversive movements for the freedom of the Latin-American republics than in recording new patents.[12] A little later the Jacksonian revolution swept away what little career merit system there was, and the factional tensions of the Civil War period completed the corruption of the civil service.

In the United States, by contrast with either Great Britain or the major European countries, we have not developed career groups of permanent civil servants who are predominantly general administrators. The British, for example, started with a permanent civil service covering the major administrative positions, and then sought to improve its efficiency and to supplement it with strong scientific and technical services. By contrast, in the United States the scientific services were the first to be developed on a nonpartisan and efficient basis.

The basic reason for this contrast, of course, is quite clear. The United States was building its government from the ground up, without the benefit of a strong center of established authority—indeed, with the purpose of preventing the development of any such center. Competing factions or parties intended to use administrative appointments either to put into effect their particular policies or, more crudely, to serve as bribes for their political supporters. This spoils system was put out of business less by the civil service reformers than by the develop-

---

12 Leonard D. White, *The Jeffersonians* (New York: The Macmillan Company, 1951), pp. 207-10.

ment of strong professional groups and of specific scientific and technical criteria for appointment to office.

It was comparatively hard to prove that the country suffered if an unqualified person became a collector of customs, or a junior diplomat, or a postal executive. It was comparatively easy to prove that it suffered if he became a public health doctor or a geodetic engineer. Moreover, there were professional bodies whose standards and *esprit de corps* gave strong moral support to those who sought to improve the public service in such scientific fields. Hence the scientific and technical positions of the government were generally the first to be taken out of politics and put on a merit basis.[13]

In part this was accomplished by developing the scientific bureaus under the wing of the military departments. Some scientists, in commenting on the history of these bureaus, argue that they would have done better if they had been entirely under the direction of civilian scientists. But I think it is probable that the military services, especially in the mid-nineteenth century, were the only parts of the federal government that could be counted on for a measure of continuity and stability in administration. As poorly as they were frequently administered, they at least were founded on the ideal of a non-partisan career system, in which provision could be made for scientific training.

West Point, it should not be forgotten, was the first engineering school in the United States, and it was the Army engineers who applied the sciences of the day to the surveying and development of the West and to the provision of internal improve-

[13] Lewis Meriam, *Public Personnel Problems* (Washington: The Brookings Institution, 1938), p. 317. ". . . the tendency has been to leave in the patronage fields the . . . general administrators. . . . Our national legislator and political executives have on the other hand repeatedly recognized that for scientific, technical, and professional work, competence in the field and permanency of tenure are essential."

ments. Similarly the Navy, with its need for skills in navigation and shipbuilding, was a natural sponsor of the sciences. The Naval Observatory was one of the earliest federal agencies to undertake the support of relatively basic science; A. A. Michelson undertook his work on measuring the velocity of light as Ensign Michelson, U.S.N.

When the civil service reform movement got under way in the latter part of the nineteenth century it was no longer possible to hope that a general civilian career service could be established. If we were to take government jobs out of politics, it could not be done by setting up a separate class of career officials. Each job had to be filled by the person who could prove that he was the best able to perform its particular duties. To withstand political criticism the examination had to be as specific and as objective as possible.

By consequence, government personnel systems in the United States had to make use to the fullest possible extent of fool-proof testing methods. The psychologists helped to introduce into government some of the most advanced techniques of testing, selection, and classification of personnel.

Some of this was useful. But a great deal of it was not, and the public personnel system bogged down in a mass of pseudo science. Recruitment examinations were devised so as to keep the examiner from having to use any judgment. The objective short-answer test prevented the examiner from being considered partial or partisan, but it did little to help him select candidates for government jobs who would have the intellectual ability to deal with general policy issues and the personal qualities that would enable them to accept managerial responsibility. Similarly, the detailed classification of positions was suitable enough for specialized and subordinate functions, but it was a great handicap to the creation of a career service in the higher ranks of research workers or administrators.

While this defect has led to great difficulties in the development of general administrators, it has left the field free for scientists and engineers to move into managerial positions. In American government, as in American business, the top executive positions have not been pre-empted either by a single social class or by a closed career service. Consequently, in all the fields in which scientific or technical knowledge is important, scientists and engineers have tended to rise into positions of executive responsibility. In Great Britain the scientific civil servants have always complained that they were kept out of positions of top authority by the administrative class. In the United States the complaint is more likely to be the opposite—that good scientists are ruined by being taken from laboratory positions and given administrative responsibilities for which they may be poorly suited.

While the American democracy distrusted public officials as a class, it was almost equally distrustful of organized science and the professions. It is worth remarking that in the United States, by contrast with Great Britain, admission to a profession is controlled by examinations administered by a government, rather than by professional societies. Similarly, American universities are not controlled by governing bodies made up of university scholars; instead, they are headed by boards of lay trustees. Accordingly, scientists and engineers of the more ambitious sort were not content to look on their profession as a separate segment of society. Instead, they moved naturally into administrative and executive positions in business as well as government, with the purpose of applying their scientific skills to practical affairs.

This system developed, no doubt, partly because there was no group of career civilian administrators in the government (as there was a group of career military officers) to maintain general control over the administration of public affairs. The lack of such general administration has probably made for poor management in little things, but for dynamic administrattion in the big issues. For it puts in positions of executive responsibility men who are committed by their training to the exploiting of new ideas and the adoption of new techniques.[14] These are not, in general, the men who judge their accomplishments by the absence of criticism and by administrative convenience. They are far more likely to fall into the opposite error, of believing that the public interest is the same as their professional specialty.

In this tendency the scientist-administrator is aided by the nature of the American federal system. Like any other specialist, he can do business with his professional counterpart at other levels of government, regardless of party or of the policy of the general administration. For example, the close relation of the public health specialists—federal, state, and local—has helped to develop their program regardless of party platforms. Personnel moves from one level of government to another, and ideas are exchanged at professional gatherings. These ties, reinforced by the system of grants-in-aid, do much to strengthen many of the programs in which scientists and technicians are involved.

The expansion of government functions over the past half century has required reforms in the organization of government as well as in its personnel. In this field, too, there has been a heavy reliance on research as a preliminary to action. States and cities throughout the country, in the early nineteenth century, adopted forms of organization that were unworkable

---

14 *Sixth Annual Report of the Advisory Council on Scientific Policy (1952-1953)* (London: H. M. Stationery Office), Cmd. 8874, p. 2. ". . . scientists and engineers are urgently needed not only in the laboratories and workshops, but also in the board rooms of British industry. . . . It is no accident that the enormous growth of American production has coincided with an increasing representation in management of men with a strong scientific or technical background."

in the society created by modern science and industry. The steps toward reform, which have made impressive changes at all levels of government, have followed painstaking research by universities and research bureaus. To the foreign visitor the most striking phenomenon in American government is likely to be the extent to which private research institutions play a continuous role in the development of government administration—a subject that in most European countries, and even in Great Britain, is considered the province of the professional civil servant alone.

The emphasis on research as a preliminary to governmental action comes, of course, from an unwillingness to permit the government not only to answer a question arbitrarily, but even to define the issue, present its views, and manage the administrative machinery. This unwillingness to take the answers from established authority leads to a tremendous use of research as a basis of decisions at all levels. The Congress itself, being unwilling merely to act on the recommendations of the President, relies on its committees. Those committees in turn do not like to trust the executive agencies to prepare the information on which they act, but make use of independent research staff. And in addition to regular staff members, the Congress has begun more and more to create special research commissions to provide it with programs on which to act.

It is a common observation among political scientists that the weakness of party discipline in the Congress makes it hard to develop a long-range and consistent policy in the United States government. It is less commonly noted that the indirect effects of the lack of Congressional discipline are as important as the direct effects, and that both reflect the American tradition of distrusting authority as such, and of wanting to handle each issue on its merits. These indirect effects are the government's lack of ability to maintain the kind of organization, staffed by the kind of career personnel, that can maintain through the years a steady and coherent view of national policy. As a result it is difficult to present general policy issues to the public and the Congress. Instead of a grand battle between opposing forces we have a series of unrelated skirmishes, generally on administrative or technical issues.

A country like Great Britain, which gradually grafted democratic institutions onto a strong system of traditional authority, could afford to let each current issue be settled by a contest between two clear-cut political parties, especially if the parties could be trusted to agree on fundamentals. But in a country that had started with a popular revolution and was only gradually developing a stable and authoritative system of government, this was a dangerous approach. The experience of the Civil War taught that lesson to those who did not already know it. As a result the American political system has not been based on a contest between two ideological systems. It has instead compartmentalized authority among Congressional committees and semi-independent executive authorities. This is a system that makes it hard to develop broad and consistent policies, while encouraging appeals to research on each separate problem.

As a result, long-range policy decisions do not depend on general political theory, but are frequently made (in effect) by groups of scientists and technicians, working in professional associations or in universities or research institutions, who develop the basic ideas to which the practical politicians will turn in order to deal with the next emergency.

In the long run this system, or lack of system, gives a great deal of influence in public affairs to men whose positions enable them to maintain a comprehensive view of new scientific and intellectual developments. Someone has facetiously remarked that our university presidents are the American equivalent of the British peerage—men whose opinions on public issues must be considered, but who have no formal power.

But for all their weight as general advisers, the university presidents are probably less influential on particular policies than the scientists who are leaders in their professional societies and research councils. De Tocqueville remarked that where you found a public enterprise headed in Great Britain by a man of rank, and in France by an agency of government, in America it would be headed by an association.

This has been particularly true for the government programs in which science is concerned. The origins of policies are not to be found in party platforms or the pronouncements of political leaders. They can rather be traced in the discussions that take place among leaders in scientific and professional fields, in the research studies that such discussions stimulate, and in the consequent consensus among the professionals.

During the twentieth century the influence of such intellectual leaders has been greatly extended by the financial backing of the great foundations. The foundation officials themselves, always on the lookout for new intellectual developments that may contribute to public affairs, thus make a great contribution in the long run to public policy. In part their influence has been exercised by supporting work aimed directly at problems of government, as did the Spelman Fund when it supported the organization of professional societies of public officials. But they have exercised even greater influence on government almost absent-mindedly, by their support of scientific and technical programs. The atom bomb might never have been developed if the Rockefeller Foundation had not built cyclotrons in the middle 1930's, or in the 1920's given financial support in Europe to Enrico Fermi and Niels Bohr. To take a less known and less spectacular example, the work of the Rockefeller Foundation's predecessor, in its efforts to combat hookworm and improve agricultural education, led to experiments in local government (and in grants-in-aid to local government) that undoubtedly paved the way for the federal-state-local relationships by which most of the modern government programs are administered.

To the scientific or rationalistic mind of the eighteenth century it made no sense to let the control of public affairs depend on a hereditary monarchy, supported by traditional political theory. The classical idea of parliamentary democracy sought to solve that problem (in Great Britain) by competition between two parties, each with its own political theory, or (on the Continent) among many parties—and the more numerous the parties, the more dogmatic their theories.

This idea is accepted by a great many American political scientists as the working model by which they criticize their own institutions. But it was a pattern that never really applied to American politics. To a people brought up to question dogmatic political theory, it seemed no better to be guided by two or a dozen party dogmas than by one—and perhaps not so safe. In the American political system the pragmatic and experimental method prevailed. This was the method in which each issue was dealt with on an experimental basis, with the views of the interested technical or professional groups having more weight than party platforms or political theories. It was a method that gave far more weight to research and to scientists, and created a more dynamic economic and political system than could have prevailed under a more orderly and authoritative approach.

As we look at the relation of government and science in the United States, we must learn to think without making use of the patterns or models taken for granted by most of the textbooks. The skepticism of traditional authority and the unwillingness to create permanent and highly professionalized organs of administration were deeply rooted in the American mind in the eighteenth century by rationalist and scientific currents of thought. In America the republican revolution was a thorough one. It did not stop with the substitution of a President for a King. It went deep into the fundamental fabric of government. As the sciences had destroyed the old unified philosophical and theological system of thought, the republican revolution in America swept away the unified apparatus of authority that had been based on that system. Thus the alliance between science and the republican revolution first destroyed, and then rebuilt on a different pattern, the forms of organization and the systems of personnel that determine the practical working of authority in the modern state.

These forces were at work in the whole Western world. But they were most influential in America. The lack of a career service of general administrators, the strength and independence of the scientific and professional specialties within government, and the close ties in each scientific and professional field between the federal specialists and their colleagues in the states whose programs are supported by federal grants—all these features worked together to set free the force of organized science and to let it shape the central government of the United States into a very different institution from its European counterparts. It is a system that has been rapidly adapted to the widespread support of scientific research and the rapid application of scientific data.

In recent years we have built on these foundations a markedly new system for the support of science—a system that has produced results as terrifying as they are effective. Whether we have at the same time developed an ability to understand where this system is going, or to control it, is another question.

II

FREEDOM
OR RESPONSIBILITY?

At the end of World War II the scientists were not only more fearful of the future than the rest of us: they were also much less impressed with their own accomplishments. The rest of us were inclined to believe that the fantastic discoveries of World War II could be continued indefinitely if only enough money were provided to pay for the research. The scientists, or many of them, were more skeptical. They were inclined to look on the startling technical achievements of World War II not as a kind of progress that could be carried on indefinitely, but as the rapid consumption of a stock pile of basic knowledge. To them our scientific resources had been depleted just as we had depleted our basic reserves of iron ore and oil. We had used up a comfortable backlog of fundamental knowledge, had diverted creative scientists into the role of engineers, and could make up for the loss only by a large-scale program for the support of basic science. For this reason, they wanted to get back to their university laboratories, and as soon as possible.

The scientists viewed with particular alarm one additional fact: that it was no longer possible for the United States to look to Europe to provide it with basic research, as it had done for nearly two centuries. The Declaration of Independence had not ended the dependence of the United States on Europe as the source of its scientific ideas. This dependence decreased only gradually. By the end of the nineteenth century the United

States had indeed generally caught up with Europe with respect to industrial organization and applied technology. But in the basic sciences America still acknowledged the leadership of Europe on the eve of World War II.

The scientists, by virtue of their training and experience, saw all this very clearly. But also perhaps by virtue of their training and experience they were less inclined to ask themselves two questions—two questions that needed to be answered if the United States government was to take on the responsibility of helping to support the basic sciences.

First, how was science to be related to public policy? This question was forced on the nation by the change in international politics that had been wrought by the scientists themselves. Aeronautics, electronics, and nuclear physics destroyed the protective barriers of mere space and made the existence of the United States dependent on the political philosophy of nations on the other side of the globe, or on her own superiority in science as applied to military measures. This dependence meant that science not only had to be supported, but also had to be organized in an effective relationship to the nation's policy-making authorities—to generals, admirals, and diplomats as well as to the President and the Congress.

Then, too, how was the government to be organized to give financial support to science? The support of the most advanced intellectual processes had traditionally been left, in the Western world, to institutions relatively independent of politics. In the Middle Ages there were the church and the ecclesiastical foundations. In later centuries the universities and research institutions may have become secular in their scientific thinking, but a faintly ecclesiastical flavor remained in their ideas about organization and their relation to the rest of society. Even when they became dependent on government for their financial support, they set themselves aside from political influence by special charters or forms of organization that were much more like monasteries than like industrial corporations.[1]

It was this stream of thought that led the most eminent scientists of America, disillusioned when the dreams of Thomas Jefferson and John Quincy Adams failed to materialize, to set up the Smithsonian and the National Academy under forms of organization mainly designed as insulation against politics, and to distrust the political pattern under which the agricultural sciences were expanded so rapidly. But it was impossible to hold rigidly to this way of thinking when the fiscal structure of society changed so as to make government the only possible agency for the large-scale support of science, just as changes in the nature of science were requiring a rapidly increasing amount of money.

Scientists who dislike the restraints of highly organized research like to remark that a truly great research worker needs only three pieces of equipment: a pencil, a piece of paper, and a brain. (The experimentalists sometimes add "string and sealing wax" to the list.) But they quote this maxim more often at academic banquets than at budget hearings. For the fact remains that, even at universities, the needs of the natural scientist for more and more elaborate and expensive laboratory equipment have given him an increasingly large share of the university budget and made him an object of envy by his colleagues in the humanities and the social sciences. And out-

1 The Council of State Governments, *Higher Education in the Forty-Eight States, a report to the Governors' Conference,* Chicago, 1952. "Generally speaking, boards established to govern state institutions of higher education appear to have two basic qualities or characteristics. First, for the most part, boards are relatively independent, not directly and immediately responsive to the voters of the states or to popularly elected central state officials. By a variety of means most of the boards are screened from the direct and immediate influence of the voters and the popularly elected officials. It is apparent that the provisions establishing them and clothing them with authority to operate state institutions of higher education deliberately intended that the boards should possess a degree of autonomy."

side the universities, in the great engineering centers and institutes of applied science, the amount of money required mounts into formidable figures.

A considerable number of social scientists have discussed these generalities in more exact terms. You can give some idea of the way in which Western Europe is no longer the main source of basic science, I suppose, by the decrease in the number of scientists who have been receiving advanced training there, by comparison with the Soviet Union and the United States—where the increase, especially in the Soviet Union, has been extremely rapid. You can make a rough measurement of the change in international politics that has been effected by science if you compute the area that may be devastated, or the number of persons who may be killed, within the first hours or days after the onset of a major war. However you may figure this one, the change that has taken place over the past century is undoubtedly an increase by geometrical progression. And you can get some idea of the changing pattern of support of science by looking at the federal budget.

We do not need here any very precise figures, and that is fortunate, for everyone who compiles statistics on this problem comes out with a somewhat different answer. A half century ago the annual federal expenditures for research and development were in the range of ten million dollars. By 1930 they were something less—perhaps considerably less—than a hundred million dollars. They reached a billion dollars by the end of World War II, and two billion about a year ago.

At the same time private industry and universities have not been reducing their expenditures. On the contrary, industry is today spending from its own funds nearly three times as much money for research and development as in 1941—which is surely an increase even allowing for inflation—and universities have probably increased expenditures from their own funds even more. Even so, the federal government now supplies more than half, and perhaps nearly two thirds, of the research and development money spent in the United States.

The reason for this increase is obvious. In 1938 the Department of Agriculture spent about a third of all federal research money. War and Navy together spent only a fifth—perhaps a little less than Commerce and Interior combined. Today, by contrast, about nine tenths of the federal money for research and development goes for military purposes, including the research programs of the Atomic Energy Commission and the National Advisory Committee for Aeronautics, and nearly three quarters of it goes to the Defense Department alone.[2]

If you have a taste for charts or graphs, you can easily picture the way our present problem has developed in the past half century by drawing three steeply mounting curves: the increase in the possibilities of immediate devastation by modern war, the increase in the amount of money the United States government is putting into scientific research, and the increase in the numbers of scientists who have been trained—or who need to be trained if we, rather than the Soviets, are to take the leadership in basic science that was held until a few years ago by Western Europe.

If you are concerned with the financial support of basic science, by contrast with engineering or development, you may well say that this is an exaggerated picture. You may argue that it is by no means certain that support for the basic sciences cannot come from private donors, including corporations and foundations. It is true, of course, that of the roughly two billion

2   For data on support before World War II, see National Resources Committee, *Research, a National Resource* (Washington: Government Printing Office, 1938), I. For current data, see National Science Foundation, *Federal Funds for Science: I. Federal Funds for Scientific Research and Development at Non-Profit Institutions, 1950-1951 and 1951-1952; II. The Federal Research and Development Budget, Fiscal Years 1952 and 1953* (Washington: Government Printing Office, 1953).

dollars that the federal government is spending each year for research and development at least nine tenths goes for applied research and development, and probably the amount for basic research is closer to three than to ten per cent. Indeed, the more conservative scientists will argue that the pressure of two billion dollars a year has forced many of our most capable scientists—the men who might be expected to provide the fundamental advances in basic science—to leave their laboratories, to become the administrators of large defense research projects, and to spend their time in committees dealing with public policy. This argument is plausible even to one who is not a scientist, if he has any appreciation of the pressure of the Pentagon on American universities to organize their best brains to support the development of weapons.

The best informed scientists argue among themselves whether the very aspects of this system that produce the most dynamic development of technology are more likely to encourage or actually to discourage the development of leaders in fundamental science.

On the hopeful side there remains the fact that American industry has spent remarkably large sums for the support of science. Much of this, of course, is not for basic research, which rarely leads directly to industrial uses, but for the development of new things that can be patented and exploited for competitive purposes.

The promotion of basic research by private donors is no longer a matter that depends entirely on personal wishes or private generosity. It has become almost as directly a matter of public policy as our federal appropriations themselves.

As one of our most eminent conservative statesmen once remarked to me, we have not socialized management in the United States, but we have socialized income. The income and inheritance tax system has greatly cut down the accumulation of individual personal fortunes. The greater potential private source of support for science and education is not the individual but the corporation. The New Jersey Superior Court recently ruled (and its decision has since been confirmed by the Supreme Court) that a private corporation could legally make a gift to a university for educational, scientific, and welfare purposes— a decision that may be an important precedent in encouraging further corporation giving.[3] Recent studies by the National Planning Association have pointed to the opportunity of private corporations to make gifts that will be exempt from corporation income taxes up to five per cent of their total income. If corporate giving ever approaches such a figure, the amount of support that it may provide for science, along with other educational and welfare causes, may be considerable.

In the past year, however, it has become clear that financial support from private sources may well be made subject to closer government regulation. In the investigation of tax-exempt foundations during 1952 by a select committee of Congress, under Representative Cox, it was obvious that the members of Congress considered that the privilege of income tax exemption put on private institutions, including foundations, an obligation to prove to the public—and specifically to the Congress— that their expenditures were in the public interest.

It is remarkable that some of the most conservative members of the Congress were those who seemed the least likely to assume that foundations, as private institutions, had a right to manage their affairs in their own way without government regulation. Their attitude toward the professional executives of the private foundations was similar enough to their attitude toward civil servants to make it clear that the ability of foun-

---

[3] *Looking Ahead* (Washington: National Planning Association) I, No. 5 (June 1953). See also Beardsley Ruml (editor), *The Manual of Corporate Giving* (Kingsport, Tenn.: Kingsport Press, Inc., 1952).

dations to maintain their programs can no longer be taken completely for granted, but depends on the policies of the Administration and the Congress.[4]

In any case the private corporation has a wide variety of causes appealing for its funds; if it chooses to support science at all, it is most likely to support some branch of applied science that may yield returns to its stockholders. And private foundations are already devoting a large share of their funds to science, and little more can be expected of them.

Moreover, there has been a conspicuous change in the interests of the major foundations, which only reflects a general change in the climate of opinion regarding the relation of science to society. A preacher like Frederick Gates and a philosopher like Wickliffe Rose—both leaders in the early days of the Rockefeller Foundation—naturally assumed that the Rockefeller fortune could best contribute to the welfare of humanity by supporting the development of science.[5] And whereas the philosopher and the theologian of a few decades ago were inclined to take this view, even the natural scientist today is more likely to think that the critical problems of humanity are problems beyond the scope of his techniques. Some of the major foundations, partly influenced by this drift of opinion and partly by the realization that the natural sciences now require more money than can be provided by any other source than government, have accordingly shifted their main emphasis to the social sciences and the humanities.

The support of science—particularly the physical and biological sciences—has apparently become a responsibility of the

---

[4] *Hearings before the Select Committee to Investigate Tax-Exempt Foundations and Comparable Organizations, November 1952, House of Representatives, Eighty-Second Congress, Second Session, on H. Res. 561* (Washington: Government Printing Office, 1953).

[5] Raymond B. Fosdick, *The Story of the Rockefeller Foundation* (New York: Harper & Brothers, 1952).

federal government. For this reason the way in which the federal government organizes to provide that support and to see that it is properly directed is now a critical issue in American government.

We discussed earlier the two main streams of thought regarding the organization of the government's interest in science—that which was responsible for the development of the agricultural sciences, and that which established the Smithsonian Institution and the National Academy of Sciences. This was an oversimplification, because it neglected the scientific work carried on in some of the regular government departments other than Agriculture. Some of this was merely a by-product of other operations—the application of engineering techniques or individual inventiveness to the problem at hand. Thus, for example, workers in the Census Bureau invented the punch card machine. But from the time the Naval Observatory was set up, the government also began to develop laboratories for systematic programs of scientific research. The most notable outside the military departments was the National Bureau of Standards, which was set up in the Treasury Department in 1901 to put into effective practice for the first time the Constitutional responsibility of the federal government for a national system of weights and measures.

After its transfer to the Department of Commerce and Labor in 1903, and especially under the leadership of Secretary of Commerce Hoover, the Bureau was developed into an agency of service to American business generally. It worked through an elaborate system of committees and trade associations in close co-operation with a great many segments of American business, and it contributed a great deal to the standardization of industrial machinery and industrial products. But whatever the influence of these committees, the Bureau was under the immediate direction of the Secretary of Commerce, and it carried on its research work directly in its own laboratories with civil service personnel. The same form of organization was generally used in the military research programs—for example, in the Naval Research Laboratory and in the aeronautics work carried on by the Army Air Forces at Wright Field.

The National Advisory Committee for Aeronautics represented an experiment with a different form of organization. It was organized as an independent agency under a governing board that included a number of scientists from private institutions, serving the government only part time. And although it later shifted to doing most of its research work in its own laboratories and its own wind tunnels, its first research project in 1915 was undertaken by a grant to a private institution—to the Massachusetts Institute of Technology, in the modest amount of $800.

At the same time leading scientists were discovering that the form of organization adopted in the National Academy of Sciences during the Civil War was too much like that of the traditional honorific societies or academies of Europe to be effective for emergency work for the government. The Academy accordingly persuaded President Wilson to issue an executive order authorizing the creation of an operating subsidiary to the Academy, the National Research Council. The Council, unlike the Academy, was free to include on its committees men who had the most to contribute, whether or not they were eminent enough to be recognized by election to the Academy. By this means the National Research Council, although its own formal membership is much smaller than that of the Academy, always has several thousand of the more eminent scientists of the country involved in its manifold activities.

The National Research Council operated during World War I mainly with funds supplied by the Rockefeller Foundation and the Carnegie Corporation. It supported wartime research at universities, and whenever such research reached the stage of practical development the Army or Navy commissioned the scientists who were doing the work and took them into government laboratories.

The Academy and the Council, although you will find them listed in the *United States Government Manual* as public agencies, receive their basic support from private sources. Their monumental building on Constitution Avenue was built for them by the Carnegie Corporation of New York, not by the federal government. And yet when the crisis of World War II arose it was the National Research Council, far more than the regular scientific bureaus of the federal government, that was the prototype for the organization on which the federal government was to build up a totally new relationship to science.

In the meantime science had created for itself a fundamentally different relationship to the technology of industry and of military affairs, and thus to the organization of society generally. In the mid-nineteenth century there was no systematic relationship between a Joseph Henry, who was developing the theory of electromagnetism in the ivory towers of Princeton University and the Smithsonian Institution, and a Thomas Edison, who was applying this theory to commercial purposes. The scientist and the inventor were two entirely different classes of people; they lived and worked in quite different institutions and took pride in being different from each other. During the twentieth century, however, all this has been changed. The process of invention by the ingenious Yankee mechanic was changed into the business of scientific development, in which organized teams of scientists—as in the great Bell or General Electric laboratories—converted new scientific theory into practical application.

Since organized science had become the mainspring of new

developments in industry, the industrial laboratory became an essential part of the organization of some of the most progressive corporations. The great accomplishment of the O.S.R.D.— the Office of Scientific Research and Development—was to translate this change in the status of science into governmental terms. The O.S.R.D. no longer accepted the principle of World War I that a sharp distinction should be made between the status of the scientist in the university, who would be expected to work on theoretical problems, and the status of the scientist or engineer in uniform, who would work on their practical application. It picked up the old pattern of the National Research Council, which was still built around the conception of the scientist insulated from the conduct of practical or political affairs, and translated it into the central machinery of government—indeed, into the Executive Office of the President of the United States. Here it became, for the government, the equivalent of the research department of an industrial corporation.

The O.S.R.D. was not the only governmental agency that conducted military research during World War II. Measured in dollars, the total volume of its research and development work was less than that of the Navy, and less than half that of the Army. But it paced the field; it brought the leading scientists of this country into wartime research and gave them the freest rein for their talents; and it developed the new patterns for the federal government's relation to science.

The stroke of genius in the organization of the O.S.R.D. was that it combined the committee-type structure, to which scientists had become accustomed in the National Research Council, with a straight-line executive structure that gave its director full administrative responsibility and immediate access to the President of the United States. The second key feature of the O.S.R.D. system was that it did not merely bring individual scientists into government service. Instead it brought scientific institutions into government programs on a wholesale basis. Let us look at these two points in a little more detail— the first in this chapter, the second in the next—for they served as the point of departure for the Manhattan District, through which the Army administered the atomic energy program, and later for the Atomic Energy Commission and for military research.

How, then, was the committee system fused with executive responsibility? The O.S.R.D. was simply a holding company under which were operated the National Defense Research Committee and the Committee for Medical Research. Men like Karl T. Compton and James B. Conant, who served under Vannevar Bush in the O.S.R.D. in a hierarchical structure, served with him in the N.D.R.C. as a committee of equals. Under them were a number of divisions, each headed by a committee of experts in a particular field. This committee structure brought together scientific colleagues from all over the United States in a form of organization to which they had been accustomed in universities and research institutions. The organization of a division was flexible enough so that its chairman could be more or less of an executive according to his energy and temperament, and much of the administrative talent of the O.S.R.D. executives was devoted to adjusting and readjusting the internal administrative relations of their several divisions.

But while the National Defense Research Committee could seem to most of its scientists like only a wartime version of their usual committee-style organization, its parent organization, the O.S.R.D., gave it a quite different effect. The President had set up only as recently as 1939 the Executive Office of the President, including an Office for Emergency Management, which was designed to give him greater flexibility in handling emergency agencies in time of war. It was in this Office for Emergency Management that the O.S.R.D. was located. As the head of an independent agency in the O.E.M., Vannevar Bush had every right to go directly to the President on issues involving the use of science and scientists during World War II. A position of direct responsibility to the President was not important mainly in order to let Dr. Bush as head of O.S.R.D. have personal conversations with President Roosevelt. It was much more important to give him the leverage he needed in dealing with the vast network of administrative relationships on which the success of a government agency depends. This is the point that is completely missed by those who think that the ideal position for a scientific agency in government is one of complete separation from the political executive.

It was this position of direct responsibility to the President, combined with his own personal qualities, that enabled Dr. Bush to deal with military leaders on equal or better than equal terms, in order to push the development of specific weapons in which leading generals were not interested. This position also let him exercise over government policies a vigorous influence that had an important effect on the use of scientists. For example, radar would never have played its timely part in World War II if Dr. Bush had not been able to exercise enough influence with the Selective Service System to protect the younger electronic experts against the operations of the draft. Nor could the whole structure of contractual relations have been maintained had he not been able to persuade the General Accounting Office to relax many of its normal peacetime rules with respect to accounting and contracts. Finally, he had to persuade the Patent Office and the Department of Justice to permit changes in patent policy in order to make industrial corporations more willing to take on the jobs of weapons development.[6]

The whole O.S.R.D. system depended, however, on an additional fact: the incentive of wartime patriotism. The scientists of the nation in wartime accepted what amounted to an informal draft, universities permitted their facilities to be commandeered and rearranged to suit national purposes, and industry went ahead with research and development without waiting to settle all the questions of patents and conflicts of interest that bothered its lawyers. Thus the war saw a great centralizing of effort in a comparatively few large facilities. The Radiation Laboratory at the Massachusetts Institute of Technology, where radar was developed, was one conspicuous example. Another was the atomic energy project, which began in the O.S.R.D. and then in its large-scale engineering phase was transferred to the Manhattan District of the Army Corps of Engineers, to be operated under the direction of a committee in which Dr. Bush and Dr. Conant were the civilian members.

The atmosphere of this system was fundamentally distasteful to the scientist. He liked being moved away from home and put on a wartime assignment, under conditions of secrecy, no better than anyone else liked military service. Yet by the end of World War II it was quite evident that the omelet could never be put back in the eggshells. Never again could the United States rely primarily for its basic science on European research. Never again could it afford to depend for its military strength on the science of other nations.

The men who had been directing the O.S.R.D. were far-sighted and realistic enough to come to this conclusion. But they were also far-sighted and realistic enough to see the problems and difficulties involved in a governmental program for

[6] Irvin Stewart, *Organizing Scientific Research for War* (Boston: Little, Brown and Company, 1948).

the postwar support of science. They were administering a streamlined and authoritative organization and using federal funds on a highly discretionary basis to support applied science for military purposes. In the long run they did not want to see federal money used only for applied research, while basic research might go begging. Even more important, they knew that the change from war to peace would pose entirely different problems of a political nature, and they were profoundly disturbed by the danger of political interference with science and by the danger of permitting a centralized bureaucracy to give money to educational and scientific institutions.

Some of the dangers of political interference with science I shall discuss in a later chapter. They are not to be dismissed lightly. And they properly played a large part in the thinking of the men who controlled the nation's most advanced scientific effort during the war, but who had no desire at the end of the war to continue their powers. On the contrary, they wished to see the country adopt a system more suitable for the support of basic science and better adapted to the protection of science in peacetime from the threats of bureaucratic control or political interference.

On the other hand, some of those interested in the general problems of organization and administration in the government naturally started with a different point of view. They believed that the government would have to go into the support of science on an entirely new scale, and that such support would make the control of research and development an important key to many issues affecting powerful interests in society. For this reason they were mainly interested in seeing that the new federal agencies for the support of research should be organized in a responsible relation to the rest of the executive branch, and particularly to the President.

These two points of view were held by two groups of men

with equal devotion to the public interest and to public service. The difference of opinion between these two groups grew naturally out of their different backgrounds and experience. One was primarily interested in maintaining the freedom of science, and the other in increasing the responsibility of the administration of government. Many of the most difficult issues in politics, like the most absorbing problems in tragic drama, come not from any simple conflict between right and wrong, but from a conflict between two conceptions of what is right.

It is this kind of issue that was posed in the legislative debates shortly after World War II over the creation of the National Science Foundation and the Atomic Energy Commission. In the proposals for these two agencies the leading scientists were convinced that the new governmental agencies, in order to protect science against political interference, ought to be insulated to some degree from the usual channels of government authority and controlled by boards of men whose principal connections were with private life. This idea drew its vitality from the traditional organization of universities and of such scientific agencies as the Smithsonian Institution and the National Academy. The other idea was that the government should support and make use of science through its regular pattern of executive organization.

The issue was first drawn in the debates over the National Science Foundation. In 1944 and 1945 Vannevar Bush prepared at the request of the President his famous report *Science—the Endless Frontier*. This report was submitted in July 1945, and its recommendations were put into legislative form in Senator Magnuson's bill to establish a National Research Foundation. Meanwhile the Subcommittee on War Mobilization of the Committee on Military Affairs, under Senator Kilgore, had begun in 1944 to consider what type of government agency should be created to maintain a high level of scientific research for the sake of national security. This subcommittee brought out its report in January and July 1945, summarizing the government's wartime research program and recommending a peacetime National Science Foundation.[7]

The differences between these two proposals were significant. Dr. Bush's report put primary emphasis on "assuring complete independence and freedom for the nature, scope, and methodology of research carried on in the institutions receiving public funds," and it sought to protect the Foundation's "discretion in the allocation of funds among such institutions." To guarantee such freedom and discretion he proposed that the Foundation should be headed by a board of nine members "not otherwise connected with the government" who would elect their principal executive officer. Finally, on patent policy, Dr. Bush emphasized that it would be necessary to give the cooperating organizations enough incentive to conduct scientific research for the government; to this end, while he wished to have the government retain a royalty-free license for governmental purposes under any patents resulting from foundation funds, he argued that the government should not require that all rights resulting from such discoveries be assigned to the government. Any such drastic requirement, he argued, would make research laboratories refuse to take federal grants to continue with work in which they had already invested a great deal of money and scientific talent.

On all three of these points Senator Kilgore and his staff held a different point of view. They took a stricter line with

[7] Vannevar Bush, *Science, the Endless Frontier, a report to the President* (Washington: Government Printing Office, 1945). See also United States Senate, Committee on Military Affairs, Subcommittee on War Mobilization, especially the following reports: *The Government's Wartime Research and Development, 1940-44* (subcommittee report No. 5, 1945); *Preliminary Report on Science Legislation: The National Science Foundation* (subcommittee report No. 7, 1945); and *Report on Science Legislation: National Science Foundation* (subcommittee report No. 8, 1946).

respect to requiring that the results of research aided by government money be free from patent restrictions. They so much feared the concentration of research in a comparatively few large institutions that they were willing (at one stage of the negotiations) to write into their legislation requirements that the research grants be distributed at least partially among the states according to some automatic formula, after the precedent of the grants to agricultural experiment stations. Most important, they differed with Dr. Bush on the form of organization by which such a program should be administered.

In the end the attempt to revise government patent policy in the National Science Foundation bill was given up. Similarly, nothing came of the idea to allocate grants proportionately by states; this was an issue on which the Bureau of the Budget, to which I was assigned at the time, sided strongly with Dr. Bush rather than with Senator Kilgore. But the issue that raised the most lively debate, and caused a Presidential veto, was organization.

The Kilgore bill provided that the Foundation be headed by an administrator appointed by the President, who would have the benefit of the advice of a part-time board, but would not be bound by such advice. This was a sharp contrast with Dr. Bush's proposal that the Foundation be headed by a part-time board that would elect its own executive.

This difference was much more than a personal difference of opinion between Senator Kilgore and Dr. Bush. Senator Kilgore developed his bill in collaboration with the Administration, and the President, on the advice of the Bureau of the Budget, was strongly of the opinion that federal funds ought not to be distributed by an agency with such a diffuse channel of responsibility as would be provided by a part-time board. On the other hand, Dr. Bush was fully supported by his colleagues and advisory committees in his decision to come out strongly in favor of having the Foundation's director appointed by the part-time board. Indeed many of the scientists, especially some of the leaders in medical education, took an even more militant stand on this issue.

The same issue was the basis of the dispute over the atomic energy legislation, even though it was obscured by some of the more vocal groups of scientists, who led the newspapers to represent the main issue as one of military versus civilian control of atomic energy.

Here the choice was between the May-Johnson bill and the MacMahon bill. The May-Johnson bill had been drafted for the Secretary of War by a committee of civilian advisers. On the issue of organization this committee had been strongly influenced by the leading figures in the O.S.R.D.—Vannevar Bush, James B. Conant, and Karl T. Compton. The MacMahon bill was drafted subsequently by staff members of the Office of War Mobilization and Reconversion and then introduced by Senator MacMahon, who became spokesman for the President and his Administration.[8]

President Truman had originally permitted the May-Johnson bill to be endorsed in the House of Representatives as a bill that represented the views of his Administration. In doing so he had apparently relied on the advice of the Secretary of War, the civilian advisers who had drafted the bill, and certain members of the White House staff. A little later, however, he reconsidered his position on the advice of the Director of the Budget and the Director of the Office of War Mobilization and Reconversion, who argued with him that under the May-Johnson bill atomic energy policy would be put in the hands of a commission virtually independent of the direction of the

[8] James Roy Newman and Byron S. Miller, *The Control of Atomic Energy* (New York: Whittlesey House, 1948), express the point of view of those who had the primary role in drafting the MacMahon bill.

President, except with respect to international affairs. This independence would be assured by a method of organization much like that proposed by Dr. Bush for the National Science Foundation—a commission of nine part-time and unpaid officials, who would be appointed one each year for nine-year overlapping terms, who could not be removed from office by the President at his discretion, and who would have authority to appoint and remove their executive director.

To Secretary of War Patterson and other sponsors of the bill this seemed a desirable arrangement, in that it would put the control of atomic energy in the hands not of politicians, but of a relatively protected group, presumably to be composed of leading industrialists and scientists. The bill conceded that international policy with respect to atomic energy should be under the direction of the President, but implied that with respect to domestic policy this part-time commission would be virtually independent.

Thus, in both the National Science Foundation and atomic energy legislation, the experience of the war persuaded many of the leading scientists that science would henceforth have to depend to a considerable extent on federal government support. But in both cases they believed that science needed to be protected from politics by being insulated from executive control by part-time governing boards.

On the other hand, it seemed clear to the President and his advisers that the same considerations that required the federal government to support science required the programs in question to be organized in the normal channels of executive responsibility. To them—or at least to some of the advisers—it seemed that the case for this point of view had been very poorly explained to the scientists, who looked on it as a means of extending political domination over science. It could be argued that the problem here was not the organization of laboratory research; that indeed each of these scientific agencies would have to decentralize its operations extensively and put them under the virtual direction of a widespread system of advisory boards. But the real problem of organization was at the top level. How was the agency going to be given the political support it needed to get the necessary appropriations? Who was going to defend the agency against political interference? And who was to represent it, and defend it, in the interdepartmental infighting that is so important in Washington?

The predominant opinion in the Bureau of the Budget, for example, was that the greater threat of political interference and patronage—whether in personnel, in contracts, or in other forms of political favors—had typically throughout all our history come less often from the President and his department heads than from local interest groups exerting pressure on members of the Congress. It was for this reason that it opposed the view, which was strongly held by some of Senator Kilgore's advisers, that the legislation creating the National Science Foundation should specify a formula for distributing grants among the states on a geographical basis.

At the same time the Bureau took the view that the firm support and leadership of the President might be needed to protect the principal scientific agencies of the government from political interference in the future. This might be particularly true, it was argued, of an agency that has the function of making grants of money to private institutions. Any board of part-time general advisers is almost necessarily drawn from the institutions that must benefit from such grants, or from among the professional colleagues of leaders in those institutions. To put such men in a position of complete executive responsibility for the program is to ask them to stand before the Appropriations Committees of Congress and defend a program of grants to themselves or to their friends. This is bad enough if the men in question are the most honorable and public-spirited leaders in their field, for it puts them in a position where they are vulnerable to unfair political attacks. It is even worse for the nation if such men refuse to serve, and if the positions in question become the objects of competition by second-raters who intend to use the positions to benefit their institutions or their fields of interest. The only protection against such an outcome was to keep the part-time advisers in positions where they were primarily advisory in function, and to leave the legal responsibility in a full-time subordinate of the President.[9]

But this was not a point of view that was persuasive to most of the scientists. On their side it may well be argued that the most effective protection of science has usually been achieved by the board form of organization; that such boards can be set up to include men of high prestige and public spirit who are not in universities or other agencies receiving grants; and that such an arrangement guarantees a type of stability—and, perhaps more important, the confidence and respect of the community of scientists—far more effectively than does a complete subordination to the Chief Executive.

I have oversimplified the problem by posing it as an issue between two sharply defined points of view. There were, of course, all sorts of variations, in part the result of normal differences in theory, in part the result of normal prejudices and selfish interests. In short, the problem was about as complicated as any other major political problem. But the issue of reconciling the objectivity and independence of science with the responsibility of the governmental system was the most important thread that ran through all the tangled argument.

In the case of the National Science Foundation, the issue

9 This was my own position at that time, as I argued in an article entitled "The Deficiencies of the National Science Foundation Bill," *Bulletin of the Atomic Scientists*, October 1947, p. 23.

was settled only after five years of Congressional debate. In one effort to compromise, the Congress in 1947 passed a bill that on most issues was satisfactory to both camps. The President vetoed the bill, however, exclusively on administrative grounds, because it put the fundamental control of the Foundation and its programs in the hands of a part-time board. The bill as finally enacted and signed in 1950 complied with the President's main terms, although it was a considerable compromise. It permitted the President to appoint the director, the principal executive of the Foundation, but it also provided that the award of contracts or fellowships had to be approved not only by the director but also by the Foundation's board of twenty-four part-time members.

On the other hand, the scientists who followed the leadership of Dr. Bush had accomplished their main purpose with respect to the substance of the program. The Congress and the public, which had started with the idea that the nation needed a special system to give bonuses or awards to inventors—at any rate, with the idea of aiding applied science—had been won over to the creation of a federal agency for the support of basic research.

In the case of the atomic energy legislation the issue of organization was settled more quickly by the influence of the Administration in the Senate. Under Senator MacMahon's leadership, with the assistance of staff work from the Office of War Mobilization and Reconversion and with vocal public support from the younger nuclear physicists, the May-Johnson Bill was set aside in favor of MacMahon's bill providing for the control of the atomic energy program by a full-time commission fully responsible to the President.

In the atomic energy program it was pretty generally agreed immediately after the war that the program should be transferred out of the War Department and into a civilian agency.

In spite of the haggling over the details of the bill, this purpose was accomplished. But the same issue, with respect to the general support of science, was not settled by any such clear-cut decision. Indeed, it was let go by default.

No one expected the proposed National Science Foundation to take over the federal government's entire interest in the support of science. All of the more influential advocates of the Foundation understood that almost every department of the government had some function that required it to support scientific research, perhaps including basic research. Everyone assumed that the scientific activities of the Department of Agriculture, of the United States Public Health Service, and of the military departments would have to continue in those agencies, in close association with the operating programs that they were designed to benefit.

This view, as reasonable as it was, complicated the political problem of establishing the National Science Foundation. In theory a member of Congress could agree that basic research was a good thing for its own sake. But this was not the kind of belief that led a member to stand up and be counted in favor of the spending of federal funds. It was not nearly so strong a belief, for example, as the conviction of a member of the Military Affairs Committee that we ought to support enough research on military weapons, or as the conviction of a member of an Agriculture committee that we ought to support research on how to improve crops or cure diseases of cattle. The individual Congressman, like most other people, could see more clearly that science was a good thing if he could see at the same time in just what way it would benefit his particular interests.

As a result there was no great political steam behind the National Science Foundation legislation. While Congress haggled over its exact terms the passage of time was settling the most important issue in the relation of the federal government to science. It permitted the military departments and the scientists to set up a program in which most of the nation's scientific effort was supported through military appropriations.

The scientists as a class always seemed to be quarreling with military officers as a class, even while they were developing one of the most effective partnerships in history. At any rate, some of them were among the most vocal advocates of civilian rather than military control in scientific matters. Yet the scientists were more successful in persuading military officers than in persuading civilian Congressmen that generous support for science was essential to national security. Early in 1946, for example, a memorandum from the Chief of Staff of the Army to the General and Special Staff and to the principal commanding generals stated that it would be the policy of the Army thereafter to give generous support to science, to give scientists "the greatest possible freedom to carry out their research," and to call on civilian scientists not only for the production of weapons but also for assistance in military planning. The Army, General Eisenhower went on to say in this memorandum, ought not to duplicate within its own organization the "industrial and technological resources" of outside organizations, which should be used "as organic parts of our military structure in time of emergency." To make such a system possible within the Army, the same memorandum went on, "we must separate responsibility for research and development from the functions of procurement, purchase, storage and distribution."[10]

This was a sharp departure from the earlier doctrine of military organization. All military services had generally be-

10 Dwight D. Eisenhower, *Memorandum for Directors and Chiefs of War Department General and Special Staff Divisions and Bureaus and the Commanding Generals of the Major Commands. Subject: Scientific and Technological Resources as Military Assets* (30 April 1946).

lieved that weapons research ought to be carried on under the direction of officers who knew what was needed in combat. This meant that military laboratories were usually located well down in the chain of command; that such laboratories, even though staffed mainly by civilians, were always headed by military officers; and that research projects were undertaken only according to the terms of a statement of "military requirements." The new policy statement by General Eisenhower meant that the scientists—especially those in the O.S.R.D.—had persuaded the military officers far more effectively than they had the Congress, even while their main purpose may have been to free science of military control.

As it had worked out in practice, the Army had actually been the slowest of the services to give research a relatively high place in its organization. After a false start in 1946, it was not until 1952 that it set up a Chief of Research and Development in the Office of the Army's Chief of Staff, who could give policy direction to the Army research programs from a higher level than the staff in G-4—the section of the General Staff that deals primarily with procurement and matériel.

In the meantime the Navy had set up the Office of Naval Research in 1946, on the same level as its historic statutory bureaus. Without taking away from those bureaus their programs of applied science, the Navy charged the O.N.R. both with carrying on research of a basic or general nature and with co-ordinating the research of the Navy as a whole. With this general mission the O.N.R. in the few years after World War II did the job that Congress was debating for the National Science Foundation: it supported a large share of the basic science of the United States. Much more to the surprise of the academic world, it did so by a system of grants and contracts carefully devised to provide a high degree of academic freedom. It was so successful in this respect that when the National Science Foundation was finally created, the chief scientist of the O.N.R. seemed the inevitable choice as director of the National Science Foundation.

Meanwhile the Air Force, which was a fighting arm that had to improvise all its supporting services when it became a separate Department, set up a Deputy Chief of Staff for Development as an independent part of its general staff structure. To carry on its operating programs it created the Air Research and Development Command and made it entirely independent of the Air Matériel Command, which had always run Air Force research as a subordinate part of its job of buying airplanes.[11]

The Army and the Air Force could not catch up with the Navy in the support of basic research, but they greatly expanded their programs in that direction, with the active support of the Research and Development Board of the Department of Defense. This board, created to help the Secretary of Defense co-ordinate the scientific programs of the military services, will come to our attention again in a later chapter.

The National Science Foundation finally got into active operation about the time of the invasion of South Korea. The expansion of military appropriations that followed the new war was more important in determining the pattern of government support for science than any amount of rational debate. In consequence the Congress was always inclined to cut down severely on the President's budget for the National Science Foundation, which was supervised by a board including some of the leading scientists and educators in the nation, even while

[11] Since this statement was written the Air Force has had (October 6, 1953) the Deputy Chief of Staff for Development report to the Deputy Chief of Staff, Matériel. Trade journals attributed this action to demands from the aircraft industry.

vastly larger sums were being distributed for precisely the same purposes by junior officers in relatively obscure corners of the military departments.

The existence of the National Science Foundation, with its statutory function "to evaluate scientific research programs undertaken by agencies of the federal government" as well as to support basic research directly, raises a crucial question with respect to the future direction of science in the federal government. To what extent should the National Science Foundation be used by the President and his Executive Office to co-ordinate in any aggressive way the scientific programs of the executive branch?

The National Science Foundation is the only general-purpose science agency in the government, and the President and the Bureau of the Budget are certain to look to it for advice on the science program as a whole. The President and the Bureau, for example, have always recommended much higher budgets for the Foundation than the Congress has been willing to appropriate. At the same time any aggressive effort at co-ordination will surely be resisted by the executive departments and agencies, all of which are certain to prefer to conduct their scientific programs in their own ways.

Similarly, especially at a time when economy is the Administration's watchword, the executive departments—particularly the military departments—will be under pressure to reduce their expenditures for any research not clearly related to their operating functions. For example, the Congress recently revised the National Science Foundation Act by removing the limitation on its appropriation. It did so in order, as the Committee on Labor and Public Welfare reported, "to permit further centralization of basic scientific research in the National Science Foundation."

Aside from natural jurisdictional prejudices, other departments have some reason to distrust this proposal. At the end
of 1951 the President reduced the budget that he was recommending for basic research in the military departments by five
million dollars and increased the National Science Foundation
budget by a similar amount. The Congress was glad to accept
the reduction in the military budget, but it struck the figure
out of the budget of the National Science Foundation as well.
Practical political experience certainly suggests that science is
more likely to receive generous support in connection with
the specific operating programs of the various departments
than if it were entirely centralized in a purely scientific agency.

But the main argument of the scientists against centralization
is one of principle, not politics. They fear that to centralize
the control of government support of research in a single
agency, no matter how wisely administered, would be a cal-
amity. Basic research is tricky and unpredictable; what one man
thinks a thoroughly useless approach may seem to another a
most promising one, and either may be right. The scientist
thinks that there is safety in a variety of agencies, with a variety
of advisory or review committees of experts, all trying in competition to discover and support the most promising basic
research.

In Great Britain the problem of giving government financial
aid to scientists in universities, without political interference,
is solved by the University Grants Committee, which distributes
public funds to universities for research, among other purposes.
This Committee, however, operates behind the shelter of His
Majesty's Government. Its funds are provided in an executive
budget that the House of Commons has not altered by so
much as one penny during the twentieth century. Its grants
are not questioned by any Appropriations Committee of the

House of Commons, because the House of Commons has no such committee.

If the United States government were organized on similar lines, science might well rely for its protection against politics, and for its political support, on an agency like the National Science Foundation. If your central executive organization is impregnable, you may well seek to prevent political interference with science by organizing under its wing a strong agency for the support of science. But if the executive organization of the government is scattered and diffuse, and if the political support of programs has to be built up in specialized executive agencies and specialized Congressional committees, then the scientific programs, too, will do well to be diversified instead of centralized. This political argument corroborates the general administrative argument that research programs and operating programs need to be guided in close co-operation with each other if both are to be made directly effective.

But if the support of science is to be thus diversified among various departments and agencies, there is all the more need for a strong National Science Foundation. Such a Foundation, with adequate funds, is badly needed to support the basic research that is not closely enough related to the interests of other agencies to attract their funds. It is needed even more to redress the balance between basic and applied research, since the operating agency will always overemphasize projects that have an immediate application in mind. America has been weak in basic scientific theory, just as she has been weak in creating a general government policy. She has been weak in both respects because in our educational system, our research programs, and our government generally we have put all our emphasis and all our financial support on the specialized application of knowledge. The development of basic science suffers from the competition of the specialized applied sciences, just as the general policies of government designed to protect the citizen and consumer are weak by comparison with the pressure group or the specialized interest, and just as the general administrative personnel of the government is weak by comparison with the specialists.

The National Science Foundation is the only agency of government that can help the President and the Congress appraise the general policies of the government with respect to science. If it discharges this mission, it will have no time to do what some scientists fear—to attempt to centralize the direction of scientific research. That is a matter that depends on the decisions in a great many universities and laboratories and in a great many agencies that finance specific research projects. In this level of operations the National Science Foundation has very little reason to meddle.

On the other hand, no other agency is in a position to look at the way in which all the specialized programs of the federal government affect science as a whole. No other is in a position to ask how the federal programs influence those of the universities and industrial laboratories and what effect they have on private sources of financing. No one else can look into the effect of government personnel policies, in all departments and agencies, on the ability of the government to carry on first-rate scientific work. And finally, no one else is in a position to inquire what branches of science need more adequate support if the American people are to maintain the fastest possible rate of technological progress, as well as the most adequate national defense, in the troubled world of the late twentieth century.

In the organization of the government for the support of science we do not need to put all science into a single agency; on the contrary, we need to see that it is infused into the program of every department and every bureau. We do not need to insulate it from executive authority; on the contrary, we shall protect it best against political interference and enable it to be most effective if we give it a direct and effective relationship with the responsible executives, as well as the support of well-organized groups of advisers from the leading private institutions of the nation.

FEDERALISM
BY CONTRACT

Socialists believe that the interests of the proletariat can be protected only if the government owns the means of production. Anarchists think that anything the government owns or does is a blow to the freedom of the individual. This theoretical issue is argued, in only slightly less extreme terms, as more and more people become aware that the federal government, and particularly the Department of Defense, has become the principal support of scientific research in the United States. The lawyers and accountants and reformers who fear the predatory private interests argue that private institutions must not be allowed to profiteer on government grants. Suspicious capitalists and scientists who are jealous of their academic freedom say that he who pays the piper calls the tune—that the government, whenever it puts funds into research, is bound to destroy the liberty and initiative of those who receive the money.

These two points of view, while superficially at opposite poles, are fundamentally in agreement. They both hold that the public interest is necessarily opposed to private interests, and that government cannot ever provide funds without destroying the independence of the institutions that receive them. But this is only another version of the idea that power is indivisible—the old idea that was the core of the theory of sovereignty as Austin explained it; the idea that is the basis of the organization of unitary states.

It is hard for this absolute idea to live in an intellectual climate conditioned by the analytical and skeptical approach of the scientist. The rudiments of the scientific approach in the age of Franklin and Jefferson helped to dissolve the traditional idea of sovereignty and to create the first large-scale federal system of government. The grant-in-aid programs that scientists helped to develop became the dynamic basis of the federal system, as it undertook in the twentieth century to meet national problems without destroying the independence of the states. And now, in the research and development programs, the scientists have brought to its most complete development an improvised system of federalism that makes use of private institutions for the conduct of federal programs. To those who argued that you cannot divide sovereignty, as to those who believed that you could not divide the atom, the answer of the scientist was simply to divide it.

The general trend of the past few years in the United States has been against socialism, and even against an expansion of the power of the federal government. In this setting it is remarkable that there have been very few complaints, even from the most touchy and suspicious scholars, to the effect that the federal government is dictating to scientists. The recent Commission on Financing Higher Education, for example, a privately supported study with a moderately conservative cast, noted the extensive federal support of science and admitted that "although there are signs of danger which have appeared in these programs they have not been serious."[1] The Commission did not advise that the present programs be stopped, but only argued that new forms of federal subsidy ought not to be adopted, particularly in the humanities and social sciences.

While there has been a great deal of criticism of detailed

---

[1] Commission on Financing Higher Education, *Nature and Needs of Higher Education* (New York: Columbia University Press, 1952), p. 157.

administrative arrangements, and some fear that universities are taking on so large a portion of federal programs that they will be seriously damaged in case of severe retrenchment, there has been no organized objection from scientists and educators to the general development of federal aid. Its absence may be taken by the cynical to be only the result of the fact that nobody shoots Santa Claus. But the more important reason is the improvised form of federalism that now governs the relations of the federal government and scientific institutions. This new system of relationships, based on the administrative contract, not only gives support to scientific institutions that yet retain their basic independence, but it also creates new ones that become equally independent.

The superficial forms under which this new system masquerades are familiar enough: they are the private corporation and the cost-plus-a-fixed-fee contract. But in the aggregate these superficial forms conceal something that is a substantially new system, and one that is not very well understood even by some of those who take part in it.

For example, in the 1953 appropriations hearings Senator McCarran, one of the more experienced legislators, undertook to criticize the research program of the Department of Defense. He asked an Air Force General who was defending the program whether any of all that money had really produced anything. The General, perhaps a little wearily, replied that the B-47 and the B-52 had managed to fly. But these, Senator McCarran insisted, were developed by private enterprise. It took some moments of discussion to point out to the Senator that the private companies that developed and built the B-47 and the B-52 had done so with the aid of Air Force research funds.[2]

[2] *Department of Defense Appropriations for 1954. Hearings before the Subcommittee of the Committee on Appropriations, U. S. Senate, Eighty-Third Congress, First Session, on H. Res. 5969. Part 2.* Thursday, June 18-Friday, July 10, 1953, pp. 1432-33.

And the Senator may never have understood that these were not invented by private enterprise in the sense that the Wrights (or was it Langley?) invented the original airplane. Neither was their invention merely paid for by the federal government, in the way in which it pays for so many trucks or typewriters. Instead, they were developed according to exacting specifications laid down by Air Force planners, which in turn were based on the best strategic decisions that the Air Staff could make on the basis of intelligence regarding the Soviet Union, the advance in aeronautical science, and the incorporation of related advances in several dozen other technical fields, such as electronics and nuclear physics.

I have said that the United States has improvised a new kind of federalism for the conduct of research. This is based on at least five types of relationships with private institutions.

The first and simplest is a contract for the improvement of a certain machine or weapon, for the development of a new one, or for any specific research project in an industrial laboratory or in a university. Some such contracts are for the production of items in quantity, with a little research on the side to improve the product. Many others are now for the improvement of the item or for more or less basic research that will lead ultimately to entirely new devices.

In contracts of this type, the very nature of the problem has forced the military agencies to develop what is called the "systems approach." They recognize that they are no longer dealing with a series of weapons more or less independent of each other, or at least easily adjusted to each other, as might have been true some decades ago when the Navy was seeking to improve its battleships and at the same time to improve the guns to be mounted on their decks. All this has been changed by modern techniques of communication, by the speed and power of modern weapons, and—most important—by the fact that scientific development is no longer a short-term job for the engineer alone, but a long-term job for a team of scientists and engineers combined.

It would not make sense, for example, to have one company develop an airplane while another was working on the bombs it was to carry. Either project might take from five to ten years, and if the jobs were actually done independently they would have to be scrapped and done all over again. For a modern bomber cannot be designed without taking into account the way in which its guns or rockets or bombs are to be carried. The navigation system that is to get it to its target and the sighting and fire control system that trains its weapons on that target have to be geared into each other and into the whole system of communications and tactical command. If all these things are to interlock with one another and into the tactical plans of the combat leaders and the production plans of the industrial mobilizers, they have to be planned as a closely knit system and developed as a system. This job can be done well only within a single integrated administrative organization.

These considerations have required the military departments to begin to set up fewer research projects for the development of particular items, and to proceed more often by parceling out to a particular contractor the development of an entire system of related weapons and devices and techniques.

This method makes it unnecessary for the military service to go through the rather clumsy process of preparing detailed specifications on a whole host of closely related items intended for future development. It puts in the hands of a much more flexible type of organization the preparation of the whole new package of related items, so that all can be developed in harmony, adjusting some to compensate for the failure of others. It also makes it possible for the military service to devote more attention to the more important or higher level job of military planning—that is to say, deciding which kinds of weapons systems will be required to meet the needs of any future war and which ones can be adopted as the basis of strategic planning within the limits of our physical and scientific resources.

These are the ways in which the traditional contracts with industrial corporations have been developed, especially by the military departments, to meet the requirements of the new military technical problems. A second and quite different type of relationship is involved in the contracts that the government makes with research laboratories and universities. Some of these are grants avowedly for the purpose of supporting scientific research for its own sake, especially those made by the National Science Foundation and the Public Health Service. Others, especially in the military departments, take the form of contracts that come to much the same thing. Indeed, the military departments have now found it unnecessary to have a contract for each new project. Instead they sign with each of a number of institutions a contract that merely states the terms of their general relationship, so that a new project can be undertaken by a simple order without further detailed negotiations or the signing of a new contract. The "master contract" is the basic charter of the new federal relationship.

The third type of relationship in this new system is the special study. From time to time the military services have identified a major problem that requires a new approach, based on a combination of scientific and strategic or tactical thinking. This is the kind of problem that has traditionally been assigned to military staffs, in the general staffs of the great powers of the past century. Only in the United States have such broad studies of crucial importance to national strategy been farmed out to private institutions.

The basic problem of defeating the submarine, the ground and air strategy for the defense of Western Europe, the tactics and weapons systems for the air defense of the United States and the protection of its civilian population—subjects like these have been analyzed for the top military authorities by private institutions working under contractual arrangements. We shall look in a later chapter at some of the problems that such studies involve.

A fourth type of relationship grew naturally out of the earlier ones. A military department saw that the development of an important new weapon or weapons system required the creation of an entirely new laboratory or plant. It understood, too, that the problem was not merely a scientific one. It required the creation of a competent and stable large-scale organization. That is to say, it required managerial competence in the conduct of a scientific enterprise. For this it turned to the major universities. The universities were willing to take on such assignments and glad enough to separate them from their regular administrative systems.

A number of universities had already discovered, to their sorrow, that the business of weapons development and related strategic studies are not only big business, but a very special kind of business that it is very difficult to mix with the traditional life of a university. It is hard to reconcile with the traditional habits of academic freedom the sentries and barred gates that are required by security regulations for some types of military research. It is hard to reconcile the fluctuating personnel requirements of emergency activity with the status and tenure of traditional faculty appointments. And the university business manager is always nervous about building into the physical or financial structure of a university a set of activities that are presumably emergency in nature and may some day be cut down sharply by political authority.

For all these reasons universities have set up separate organizations for much of their military work. The Argonne

Laboratory at the University of Chicago, supported by the Atomic Energy Commission, now has a budget larger than that of the entire university before the war. The Lincoln Laboratory at the Massachusetts Institute of Technology now spends close to $20,000,000 a year, which is much more than the Institute spends on teaching its students. The Applied Physics Laboratory of John Hopkins manages a research program for the Navy that involves subcontracts with several dozen academic institutions.

In some cases, of course, these institutions are attached to universities only in the loosest fashion, for administrative purposes, and the federal government owns most or all of the real estate. Thus the University of California manages the Los Alamos Laboratory in New Mexico, which produced the first atomic bomb. In other cases the institutions are fairly closely associated with the ordinary university community. But in every case the military department or other agency has the advantage of buying not only scientific talent, but, even more important, the institutional ability to organize and administer a scientific program.

Finally, there are the special private corporations founded entirely for the purpose of carrying on governmental scientific programs. These show the new system in its full flower; they do not represent the mere addition of some government business to an existing institution, but are a new and more flexible method for organizing the management of public affairs. In my early days in Washington, when annoyed by the clumsiness of government red tape, I used to propose facetiously that certain government departments could be organized and managed efficiently only if they were officially abolished as such and then privately incorporated in Delaware, but at that time I did not have the imagination to see that almost exactly this procedure would be followed.

Thus, a large share of the Atomic Energy Commission's research program is delegated to a special contractor, Associated Universities, Inc., which was created for the purpose of administering atomic energy laboratories on Long Island. Thus, ARO, Inc., was created for the purpose of taking over for the Air Force the management of its great experimental wind tunnels at Tullahoma, Tennessee. And thus the Rand Corporation was created to carry on for the Air Force some of its most advanced research on the problems and techniques of intercontinental warfare.

We have, accordingly, a whole spectrum of forms of organization. This spectrum begins with a simple addition of a small research or testing project to a production contract in private industry or to a research program in a university. It goes on through various intermediate forms to the special corporation that exists solely to do research and development for the government. In total it constitutes a new and rather unsystematic system of improvised federalism, the significance of which it will take years to appraise.

But even now several major points about it seem quite clear. None of these points gives much comfort to those who want to draw a hard and fast line between government and private institutions, either in order to prevent government control of business and science or in order to prevent any businessman or scientist from profiting from work for the government.

One point is that, in the evolution of this system toward the creation of larger contracting projects, the independence of the private contractor and the scientist has increased. The contractual system makes it theoretically possible, of course, for the contracting officer to dominate completely the decisions of the contractor. He may insist on reviewing all the details of the salary he pays each employee, and the details of his research programs. It seems to me significant that this appears to happen less often as the research projects and agencies grow in size. The company with a small development project or the professor with a small research program may have reason to complain that the contracting officer does not give him enough freedom. But the large study projects and the great special corporations become organisms each with a will of its own.

The Applied Physics Laboratory has not merely worked according to military requirements: it has originated ideas that have influenced the Navy's planners in their notions about the weapons that should be developed. The Rand Corporation, in the eyes of the Air Force, has the merit of providing a thoroughly independent point of view about many issues of fundamental strategy. And through such studies as the East River Project, as we shall see in more detail a little later, corporations like Associated Universities and institutions like the Lincoln Laboratory have provided—as a part of their service under contracts with the government—some of the most vigorous and effective criticism of the fundamental policies of the Department of Defense, and indeed of the Administration as a whole.

Another point is that this system became dynamic and effective simply because it ignored the rigid distinction between public and private affairs. The new system started on a large scale with the O.S.R.D., was further developed in the Manhattan District when the Army set up that organization to take over atomic research from O.S.R.D., and was then continued after the war when the military departments took over some of the O.S.R.D. programs and the Atomic Energy Commission succeeded the Manhattan District.

But perhaps there is a more useful explanation—one that

will help us understand the remarkable speed with which this new system took hold.

The system or systems that it replaced were fairly static affairs. There were the pure scientists in the Smithsonian and a few other similar institutions; they were supported by the same board and (in part) by the same appropriations that maintained the museums and the zoo, and in recent years they have not seemed likely to have any more dynamic relation to current political problems. Then there were various specialized scientific bureaus, some (like the Bureau of Standards) under civil service, others (like Public Health and the Coast and Geodetic Survey) under special career and commissioned services of their own, but all held down to programs that looked fairly routine to the more advanced scientists in universities or industrial laboratories. Finally, there was the special world of agriculture, where research programs had been spread and multiplied by the grants-in-aid system to an extent that was unique by comparison either with other government programs in the United States or with similar programs in other countries.

But even this agricultural program was in several ways limited in its potentialities for growth. It dealt with a specialized subject matter, set aside from the more dynamic elements of industrial development that were rapidly urbanizing the nation and changing its relations with the rest of the world. Because of the very nature of its subject matter its projects and programs were relatively small and individual in scale. The scientists concerned were on the payroll of state governments and of public universities. The jealous supervision of state legislatures therefore kept down their salaries and the attractiveness of their careers; they remained a good recruiting ground for the United States Department of Agriculture, but could not have competed, even if their subject matter had overlapped, with the world of industrial science. Finally, since their programs were administered through the channels of federal-state relationships, those programs came under the close scrutiny of Congressmen interested in what went on between Washington and their respective states—a type of interest likely, within modest limits, to keep appropriations up, but discouraging to bold, ambitious national planning.

By comparison with these relatively static systems the federalism improvised by the O.S.R.D. and its successors was full of dynamic motives.

First of all there was the general structure of careers in American life. In American business, as in American government, there was no separate class of top administrators or managers from which by tradition or by family connections the scientist and the engineer were excluded. Scientists were therefore accustomed to going on to administrative and executive positions. Similarly, in American universities, many scientists had gone on to university administration, or to head special laboratories or research institutes, and in both cases they were accustomed to negotiate with business corporations or foundations as the source of funds. Both industrial corporations and universities therefore offered top careers, with ample security and high prestige, to the scientist or engineer willing to add administrative responsibilities to his scientific background.

By contrast the personnel policy of the federal government restricted to a handful the number of higher positions open to career personnel and kept these in relatively specialized categories at comparatively low salaries.

The science of economics is founded on the assumption that, in the free play of the market, the buyer will buy where he can get more for less money, and the seller will sell where

he can get the most for his product. The science of administration, which too many people think of in terms of organization charts, ought instead to be thought of as one based primarily on the choices that men make in selecting and developing their careers. In this respect, regardless of the preference of
a surprisingly large minority of capable scientists for government service, statistical probabilities were all weighted in
favor of the university and the industrial laboratory—weighted
by considerations of security and prestige if not by the amounts
of salary as well.

When it became necessary to bring the country's leading
scientists into the war program, it was far easier, and less
disturbing to all of the career relationships involved, to make
arrangements with the existing companies and institutions than
to bring the individual scientists in as government employees.
After V-J Day, when the incentive of wartime patriotism was
gone, it was all the more necessary to make the same choice.
As soon as this choice was made its dynamic features became
evident by contrast with the previous systems of government
support of science.

First of all, as the scientists eagerly left special military work
to go back to their industrial laboratories or universities, the
necessity of using private careers for public purposes became
all the more evident. It was easy enough to say that certain
defense research had to be continued. But the scientist, like
the common soldier, wanted to get back to his home institution. The contractual system made it possible to have government work done under private salary scales, with none of the
civil service red tape, without the restrictions of personnel
ceilings, and with a greater appearance of long-term security.

The system was comparable in some ways with that of the
agricultural grants-in-aid program. But there had been endless
Congressional haggling over the question whether any given

state should be permitted to have more than one experiment station in the federal program and over rigid statutory formulas for the distribution of research grants among the states. By contrast, here was a system in which the federal agencies could do business not only with state government agencies, but with private universities and industrial corporations as well.

In addition, it gave the federal agency, with whatever private help it might muster, the advantages of flexibility and initiative. The Department of Agriculture could not create a new state, but the Air Force could bring about the creation of a new corporation. The new system was an absolute necessity for the Air Force as it sought to build up the various supporting services that had formerly been provided for it by the Army. It simply did not have time to create new government laboratories in competition with the Army and Navy; it proceeded to rent them ready-made, by the contractual method.

Finally, in doing business with such institutions, there was the great advantage that the administrative channels did not correspond to political constituencies, as they did in the agricultural system. That is to say, the A.E.C. could deal with Monsanto, or the Air Force with Rand, with no Senator from Monsanto or Congressman from Rand to influence their planning. This advantage freed the executive agencies from the traditional necessity of dividing up the funds according to some statutory formula or some fixed quota for each of the several states.

In short, this new system is one that almost wipes out the distinction between public and private affairs and gives great segments of industry and education a stake in federal programs. This varies, of course, according to the degree to which any particular industry or academic discipline is dependent on federal support. Such dependence is probably greatest in the aircraft industry, which relies on federal funds to pay for nearly nine tenths of all its research and development.[3] Much the same thing is true of the fields of physics and chemistry in the universities and research institutions. As John D. Millett pointed out after directing a study for the Commission on Financing Higher Education:

> Indeed, it is no exaggeration to say that since 1940 federal contract-research income alone has enabled higher education to advance notably its research activities in the physical sciences. There is scarcely a first-rate physics or chemistry department providing graduate instruction in our universities which could maintain its present standing or personnel without federal income.[4]

In private industry the development programs and the production programs are so closely connected that it is hard to distinguish between their political effects. But in every one of the recurrent efforts to cut down on appropriations for the Air Force, the Air Force Association and the related trade associations are pretty sure to stand up and be counted in support of Air Force objectives. And not the least of their influence comes from the fact that, to the conservative Congressman, they are speaking in behalf of private enterprise rather than of civil servants.

It would be the greatest of mistakes, however, to think that most of the willingness of leading scientists to take part in this partnership with the government was the result only of their desire for federal funds. The scientific specialist is impressed by the possibility of advancing his particular field of research. A corporation manager may have an even better opportunity to

---

[3] Department of Labor, Bureau of Labor Statistics, and Department of Defense, Research and Development Board, *Industrial Research and Development, a Preliminary Report,* January 1953, p. 11.

[4] John D. Millett, *Financing Higher Education in the United States* (New York: Columbia University Press, 1952) , pp. 354-55.

make money in competitive private business; the university administrator may be able to get grants equally well from private corporations or foundations. What is likely to appeal to both of them is a combination of patriotic sentiment plus the interest and excitement of taking part in the greatest and most challenging enterprise of the age—an organized effort that makes any private program, even the dealings of the greatest captains of industry, look trifling by comparison.

This organized effort could not have been possible if the parties on the opposite sides of the table, in the negotiation of contracts, had been thinking only in terms of conflicts of interest. There were conflicts of interest, no doubt, and cases in which private institutions abused the purposes of government contracts for their own ends. But generally the managers of private institutions and public officials worked together to create a new system in which the needs of the program as a whole dictated the basic decisions. The principal issues in these negotiations did not arise between government as such and private institutions as such; they were more likely to arise between the lawyers and the administrators, or the administrators and the scientists, or the scientists and the security officers, no matter which side they worked for.

For example, the development of the contractual system for research required endless negotiations to make government contracts less burdensome on universities. The form of government contracts was designed primarily to protect the government in its relations with industry. It was necessary to work out an entirely different system to fit the quite different forms of organization and systems of accounting and personnel in the universities.

This effort required the business managers of universities to become experts in the most detailed aspects of government red tape, and it required public officials—especially military officers—to learn a great deal about private universities. They worked together in various unofficial teams and official advisory bodies. The Research and Development Board, for example, had an Advisory Committee during 1951 and 1952 on the contractual procedures covering relationships with educational institutions, with members from the military departments and from the executive staffs of universities.[5]

Let me give two examples of ways in which this committee, and others like it, were likely to find that their main issues were not issues on which public and private interests were actually in conflict, but were much like the administrative issues that arise within any large and complex system.

Take the problem, for example, of the amount of overhead that should be included in a research contract. Many universities have been willing to take grants from foundations for research projects that were barely enough to pay salaries of the scientists involved, though they then had to carry the entire burden of overhead costs themselves. This was a workable system, even with some government grants or contracts, as long as such funds represented only a small addition to the university's budget. But when the research programs multiplied in cost any such practice became impossible, and it was obviously necessary for the government to pay substantially all the costs that could fairly be charged against a project. But the calculation of such costs between a government contracting officer and a university scientist poses a constant problem. Strangely enough, it was a problem not because the university scientist always wanted more money for overhead, but because he usually wanted less. He was often convinced (and it was sometimes true) that a certain amount of money had been ear-

[5] Department of Defense, Research and Development Board, *A Review of Current Problems in Contractual Procedures Affecting Relationships between the Department of Defense and Educational Institutions*. RDB 124/24, 10 November 1952.

marked for this particular project by, let us say, the Office of Naval Research, and the less the government earmarked out of this amount for overhead to the university, the greater the amount that would go directly to the Department of Physics.[6] The only trouble with this line of reasoning was that, if generally applied, it would bankrupt universities all over the country. This alliance of the specialists at different levels against the administrators who were their respective superiors is very similar to problems in technical supervision that are found within a single large administrative organization.

A second problem on which relationships turned topsy-turvy was that of security clearance. On many types of research, of course, the university typically wanted the government agency to leave the scientist completely free of security restrictions. This is understandable enough. But on types of research that clearly called for secrecy the university did not want to be given authority to make decisions with respect to the loyalty and security of the personnel to work on the job. On the contrary, it wanted this discretion, and the accompanying responsibility, to be clearly in the hands of the public official.

This issue took shape early in 1952 while the Defense Department was revising its Industrial Security Manual. It is customary for a military department to require an industrial contractor to investigate its own personnel and to clear them or refuse to clear them for access to the lower grades of security material—those labeled restricted or confidential. Otherwise the investigating machinery of the military departments themselves

---

6 "Faculty members, as recipients of grants and contracts, tend toward the view that allowances for indirect costs reduce the funds for research support in their departments and thus they favor little or no allowance." *A Memorandum to the Executive Committee, National Science Board (National Science Foundation). Subject: Indirect Costs of Research at Institutions of Higher Learning* (20 October 1952).

would be greatly overloaded. Industrial corporations, with their personnel departments, are able to take on this responsibility; some of them may even be willing enough to have this excuse to investigate their employees.

But the possibility of requiring a university to do the same thing threatened to rock every major campus in America. For this would require a university administration, which must be committed to the idea of academic freedom, to investigate its faculty members and to decide, inevitably using their political opinions as one of the criteria, which of them could be employed on certain types of research.

It was only after sharp arguments in the top councils of the Department of Defense, and after frantic telephone calls had come in from various university presidents, that the Defense security regulations were revised so as to make the military departments take full responsibility for all security investigations and clearances among university personnel.

Some of the issues that have arisen in the government support of research have been handled, as I have said, much like the managerial issues that arise within any large administrative organization. It is a great temptation to assume that this will always be generally true—that no problems will arise in the government support of research by the contractual method that cannot be solved by reasonable men, devoted to a common purpose, in frank discussion around a conference table.

I fear, however, that this will not be true. Whenever any program requires so much money and involves the fate of so many competing institutions—industrial as well as academic—that program is certain to become loaded with political issues. That is to say, some of its principal issues will not be settled by men whose purpose is to reach a rational agreement based on compromise. They will be settled by a contest for political power, in which each side will make use of its arguments, not to convince the other side, but to win political power for itself and its friends.

Scientists generally dislike this possibility. It is for this reason that so many of them prefer forms of administrative organization that discourage the appeal to politics. Nevertheless, if the issues are such that they will inevitably become a part of the political struggle, there are strong reasons for seeing that they are considered and decided through responsible executive and legislative processes.

Several issues are already arising that will almost certainly be impossible to settle except by the decision of politically responsible executives or by legislative action.

One such issue is whether private ownership shall be given a greater role in the development of atomic energy for industrial purposes. This possibility has led a great many scientists, industrialists, and government officials to argue for giving private ownership more scope in the atomic energy business. The original Atomic Energy Act, of course, provided for complete government ownership and control of fissionable materials.

The nature of the contractual system under which the Atomic Energy Commission has carried out its program has led some important people to line up on this issue in surprising ways. David Lilienthal, who as Chairman of the Tennessee Valley Authority fought the private utilities and argued that the public needed a yardstick of government ownership in order to test the efficiency of the privately owned utilities, was persuaded by his experience as Chairman of the Atomic Energy Commission to take a stand that is superficially, at least, in the opposite direction. He now argues that our efficiency in the field of atomic energy can be maintained only by permitting big corporations to play a more active and competitive role in atomic energy matters.

Many others are now persuaded that the policy of the 1946 Atomic Energy Act has been made obsolete by two developments: the discovery of greater sources of raw material for atomic energy, and the possibility that at some time in the future the United States will have available a supply of atomic munitions adequate for military purposes. Nevertheless General Leslie R. Groves, who headed the atomic energy work in the Manhattan project, warns that it will be a most difficult task to develop atomic power for industrial uses without danger to our national security.[7]

A couple of the members of the Atomic Energy Commission have issued similar warnings. Dr. Henry D. Smyth, for example, insists that "we cannot split the atomic energy industry in two parts, labeling one for military purposes and keeping it under Government control, and labeling the other for civilian purposes and releasing it to private industry."[8] Dr. Smyth goes on to raise such difficult questions as these: How will the government dispose of the plants that it has built with the taxpayers' money? What payment would private companies make to the government in return for the knowledge and experience they have acquired as operating contractors? When do new ideas and inventions cease to be the property of the American public and become subject to patents by private companies? Finally, who would pay for the continuing research that is necessary?

[7] Leslie R. Groves, "Research—Its Goal in Industry," *Journal of the Franklin Institute*, CCLVI, No. 1 (July 1953).

[8] Remarks Prepared by Henry D. Smyth, Member, United States Atomic Energy Commission, for Delivery Before the Western Division of the American Mining Congress at Denver, Colorado, September 25, 1952, printed in *Atomic Power and Private Enterprise*, Joint Committee on Atomic Energy, December 1952, p. 101.

Even some of the most ardent advocates of the extension of private ownership in the atomic energy field recognize that the use of government loans and subsidies might lead to "the formation of new monopolies more powerful than any we have known in our generation."[9] It is therefore not surprising that the C.I.O., at its 1953 meeting, passed a resolution not only demanding that the ownership of atomic energy be kept in federal hands, but deploring the transfer of operating responsibilities, through the contractual method, to "private monopolistic corporations."[10]

As it becomes more and more obvious that the research and development of today will determine tomorrow not only the security of the nation, but also the fate of major industries, it is inevitable that the system for the support of research will be drawn more and more into the arena of political controversy. It is even more certain that political critics will become more and more alert to possible cases of conflict of interest—cases in which those whose institutions are supported by government funds have an opportunity to influence the distribution of funds and the determination of policies.

Such issues will no doubt come up in their most controversial form in industry. Nevertheless they are also likely to come up in the academic world.

This is not because, in general terms, university administrators like to receive support from federal funds. Nearly all of them share to some degree views expressed last summer by Merle A. Tuve of the Carnegie Institution, who directed the development of the proximity fuse during World War II. Dr. Tuve said that all universities should get out of the weapons business entirely; that the conduct of secret research has no

9 James N. Irwin, "Industry Bids for Atomic Power," *Harvard Business Review*, XXXI, No. 4 (July-August 1953), p. 48.
10 James N. Irwin, "Industry Bids for Atomic Power," *ibid.*, p. 39.

place on a university campus; and that the dependence of science on government support, or on any support (even that of foundations) vulnerable to political pressure, is a betrayal of science.[11]

But most university administrators, even while they are worried by these same considerations, come generally to the same conclusion as the Commission on Financing Higher Education; they would prefer not to have to live off federal funds, but they see no alternative. In this they are somewhat in the position of the young lady from Kent in the classic limerick:

> There was a young lady from Kent
> Who said that she knew what it meant
> When men took her to dine,
> Gave her cocktails and wine,
> She knew what it meant—but she went.

The first political issue likely to arise is the industrial firm versus the university. This is, in the nature of things, not an argument that it is possible to document. But there has been persistent criticism for a good many years by industrialists who resent the fact that a number of universities have been entrusted with the management of major development and engineering contracts. They argue that, since universities generally enjoy tax exemption, this is bad public policy and unfair competition with private enterprise. There are sound administrative reasons, however, for continuing to entrust major engineering contracts to universities. Perhaps the most important is the fact that most projects of this sort require a great deal of supporting work from private companies. Arrangements for such work are usually in the form of subcontracts. As a practical matter, the University of Chicago or Cal Tech may

[11] Speech at Institute of Public Affairs, University of Virginia, reprinted in *Bulletin of the Atomic Scientists*, IX, No. 8 (October 1953), p. 290.

find it easier than an industrial corporation to get industries to co-operate through subcontracts. Any advanced research and development work involves a number of trade secrets as well as secret security information, and a corporation is much more likely to co-operate with a university than with an industrial competitor.

An issue which is even more certain to arise from time to time is the issue of the small colleges and universities against the large ones, or those in the South and West against those in the Northeast. The Board of Control for Southern Regional Education, for example, undertook in 1951 and 1952 to help its member universities set up a more effective relationship with the government agencies that had funds for research contracts. In addition to a program of informing its members of the new federal programs for the support of research, the Board established an office in Washington to help Southern universities get in touch with federal research agencies. The office was closed in 1953, partly because the Board considered that the principal objectives of putting its members in touch with federal agencies had been attained, and perhaps partly because it felt hopeless about effecting a substantial change in federal research policies.

Congressmen from the South and West are naturally sympathetic to the interests of the universities in their states. They are equally likely to be suspicious that the federal award of grants and contracts is dominated by advisers from the larger metropolitan areas. This point of view was implicit, for example, in the questions that one Southern Senator addressed to the Department of Defense in the spring and summer of 1952. He asked the Secretary of Defense to inform him in detail not only about the distribution of contracts among universities, but also about the membership of the advisory groups on whose advice contracts were awarded.

The Department of Defense obviously had to acknowledge that the Defense research contracts were concentrated in a comparatively small number of large institutions. If you look at the way research and development contracts were distributed among educational institutions in fiscal year 1951-1952, you see this concentration plainly illustrated. The Defense Department, for example, put 63 per cent of its research and development funds in ten institutions; the Atomic Energy Commission put 88 per cent in the same number.

Faced with criticism on this subject, government agencies argued that the funds are placed where men are available to do the work. They point to the fact that the concentration of funds is not much greater than the concentration of advanced scientific training and graduate student enrollment.[12] And the Department of Defense, which is always under political pressure to convert money appropriated for defense purposes to other objectives, stands firmly on its cardinal principle: it does not make research contracts for the purpose of supporting science, but only "in order to get results that will strengthen the national defense, and not as a contribution to higher education."

Political issues like these face us with danger at two opposite extremes. One is the danger that individual firms and institutions will make use of political influence to gain too large a share of federal grants, or—much more likely—gain special privileges through access to secret information and special working relationships. The opposite danger, at least as real, is that the Congress may seek to avoid local favoritism by destroying the discretionary nature of the contractual system, thus leading to the award of research and development con-

[12] National Science Foundation, *Federal Funds for Science: I. Federal Funds for Scientific Research and Development at Non-Profit Institutions 1950-1951 and 1951-1952* (Washington: Government Printing Office, 1953).

tracts on the same basis on which the United States Corps of Engineers co-operates with the Congress in planning its program of building dams and levees.

This second danger becomes all the more evident if we recall that a couple of decades ago the government corporation was invented as a form of organization in order to administer government programs with flexibility and initiative and with freedom from red tape. The flexibility of the government corporations has been steadily whittled away, so that today they are as thoroughly subject to the routine budgetary and personnel controls as any government bureau.

It is, of course, perfectly possible for the same thing to happen in the framework of the contractual system. The contracting bureau can formally apply all sorts of restrictions and regulations on the private institution, in as burdensome degree of detail as it may wish. It can regulate the salaries to be paid; it can require a detailed system of property accountability; it can impose its own security regulations. Perhaps most drastic of all, it can threaten to terminate the contract. The discretion of a government bureau in terminating a contract with a private agency and later making a new contract with another is much greater than its ability to abolish a subordinate division.

Nevertheless, it does not seem likely that any such degree of control will be imposed in the near future within this contractual system. For one reason, the symbolic difference between the public and the private institution is a strong protection against undue government control. The louder you hear a group of state governments or private corporations complaining about federal control, the more evidence it is that they are relatively independent of it.

This is a matter not merely of symbolism, but of the weight of prestige and expertise, based on the marked differences in the structure of salaries and careers between public and private institutions. In routine procedural matters the contracting or accounting officer may annoy the business manager of a university in endless petty details and make his decisions stick. But on the really important issues the head of a university laboratory, or the president of the university, can appeal to echelons high enough in the government structure—and with much more authority and influence than any subordinate civil servant would have—to win his point and defend his independence.

Finally, this distinction is enforced by the attitudes of Congressional committees. If you read the hearings of the appropriations subcommittees of the Congress, you will be struck by their tendency to quibble in endless detail over appropriations for the payment of a handful of clerks and janitors on the government payroll, and by contrast their willingness to pass on great sums of money to pay the salaries of thousands of comparatively high-salaried personnel—as long as those sums go into contracts with private industry. A Congressman generally considers it his duty to assume that there may be incredible mismanagement in a government agency, but a contract with a great corporation is a prima-facie proof that the job will be done efficiently.

The contractual system has merged the public and private interest so thoroughly that the old canons of conflict of interest hardly apply. If you look at the great research programs that the aircraft or electronics companies are carrying on with government funds, your views on this relationship are likely to depend on the basic question that you ask. If you ask, from the traditional "reform" point of view, whether the private company is making too much out of a government contract, you are likely to conclude that it is guaranteeing its advancement in a fast-moving new field in a way that will keep it ahead of its competitors and help it to build up its organization at the expense of the government. If, on the other hand, you look at it from the point of view of the private manager, the company is putting at the government's disposal a vast accumulation of expertise and the managerial assets of a going concern—qualities that the government could not possibly provide for itself—and all at the risk that a change in government policy will leave the company in a poor competitive position in its traditional commercial fields.

The contractual system has certainly given the government, and particularly the military departments, great advantages of flexibility, and it has enabled them to make use of managerial talent that under present conditions cannot be found in adequate quantity in government agencies. But this very advantage suggests the major weakness of the system: a government that cannot provide adequate administrators for the comparatively minor operating subdivisions of its program is bound to have difficulty in tying those pieces together into a general program that makes sense. It is proper enough to insist that each private institution ought to be given wide latitude in a research or development contract and not be bound by unnecessary specifications or requirements. But in a broad sense the program must be based on a coherent system of governmental requirements and public policy, or there is no justification in supporting it with public funds. The basic question is whether the government has an adequate system of top management and enough foresight and expertise in preparing its advance plans to unify the vast scientific program into a coherent whole.

If we consider the necessity of shaping into a coherent whole even a minimum program of government with respect to science, we must see how much the pressure of events and the development of technology have outrun our administrative capabilities. For example, no one would wish to take away from government its Constitutional responsibility for the development of physical standards to serve as the basis of, first, fair dealing in commerce and, second, of standardization in industry. But the job of creating uniform standards is vastly more complex today than the job as John Quincy Adams saw it, which was simply to determine precisely the weight of a pound and the length of a yard. It is even more complex than in the days when Secretary of Commerce Hoover did so much to lead industries to co-operate with the National Bureau of Standards to put their technology on a uniform national basis —a program that had immense benefits for the nation's productivity. This job now requires the government to develop the techniques of basic instrumentation, which in the long run can have a profound effect on the future of science in America. The development of telemetering, of electronic chronographs, and of digital computers—and a number of other specialized instruments as well—must be undertaken by the government as the basis of the nation's research programs.[13]

But if the government is to be aware of the significance of its research grants and contracts and is to develop them in ways that will not only avoid the more dangerous political pitfalls but be a constructive influence as well, it must have more nearly adequate administrative machinery than is now available. This is partly a matter of creating a stable organization, based on attractive careers for public officials. It is also partly a problem of educating men who combine some appreciation of scientific problems with an understanding of the problems of policy and administration in a government setting.

In the comparatively narrow but advanced field of control systems some observers now recognize that engineers will have to be trained by a new kind of educational program. "A systems engineer cannot be trained by simply adding together the old

[13] Allen V. Astin, "Federal Interest in Instrumentation," a talk given at the Instrumentation Symposium, Michigan State College, March 20, 1953.

specialties. What is wanted is not a jack-of-all-trades but a master of a new trade, and this will require a new synthesis of studies. It will call for advanced work in the fields of mathematics, physics, chemistry, measurements, communications and electronics, servo-mechanisms, energy conversion, thermodynamics and computational techniques."[14]

The same observers note that industrial management must also raise its thinking to this "systems level." They might well have gone on to say that the problem of the government planner and administrator is infinitely more complex than that of the industrial manager. He has to consider not only the scientific and engineering and commercial systems, but also how they may be managed in relation to political, legal, economic, and diplomatic problems. What effect this need has on the nature of our administrative machinery, we may now try to explore.

[14] Gordon S. Brown and Donald P. Campbell, "Control Systems," *Scientific American*, September 1952.

IV

SECURITY

AND PUBLICITY RISKS

Laurence Sterne was hardly a sociologist or political scientist. But if you wish to measure the great social gulf between the eighteenth and twentieth centuries, you can do no better than to read *A Sentimental Journey*. As you do so you should remember how Sherlock Holmes solved one of his most difficult cases, not by discovering the existence of evidence but by noting its absence—the dog had failed to bark. For it is a kind of negative evidence we find in the *Sentimental Journey*.

Sterne's English traveler is in Paris. He has had a great many pleasant adventures with all classes of French people—nobles and military officers as well as innkeepers—along the road from Calais, even while observing with disdain the oppressive French political system. He has taken us, indeed, halfway through the book before he makes this remark: "I had left London with so much precipitation, that it never entered my mind that we were at war with France."

It takes some little effort to imagine that nothing out-of-the-way would happen to an Englishman traveling openly and amiably in France while England and France were at war with each other. It takes even more to imagine that the Englishman, in such circumstances, could still think of France rather contemptuously as a despotic country. But unless we make that effort we can hardly imagine the strain to which science has been put by the turn of events of the twentieth century.

For American scientists are still struggling to reconcile their eighteenth-century devotion to science as a system of objective and dispassionate search for knowledge and as a means for furthering the welfare of mankind in general, with the twentieth-century necessity of using science as a means for strengthening the military power of the United States.

To get another point of departure for our comparison let us look back to the time when the United Colonies were engaged in the war for independence. It was in 1780, during this war with Great Britain, that the Continental Congress chartered the American Philosophical Society. This Congressional charter provided that "whereas nations truly civilized . . . will never wage war with the arts and sciences" the American Philosophical Society should be free even in time of war to correspond with scientists and scientific societies in other countries, provided only that their correspondence should be open to inspection by the Supreme Executive Council of this Commonwealth.

It is important to recall that the term "philosophical" at that time did not mean one among many academic disciplines. It was a vestige from the time, a century or two earlier, when all the sciences were thought of as merely subdivisions of a single harmonizing body of knowledge, philosophy. The term persisted even though during the seventeenth and eighteenth centuries the reality had dissolved. From the time when Francis Bacon outlined the experimental and inductive process, perhaps even from the time when William of Occam denied that philosophical abstractions were living realities that could control the various aspects of knowledge, each branch of science had begun to assert its independence of general philosophy and theology.

With this movement toward intellectual specialization went a parallel development in the practical support of scholarship.

As the various branches of science became independent of theology they began to be supported in institutions independent of the church. National academies, royal societies, and the like became independent sources of scientific progress, while the universities—still handicapped by their ties with established churches—stagnated until the nineteenth century. By the time of the eighteenth-century Enlightenment it seemed clear to most rational men that man would progress the most certainly if freed from central authority of all kinds. Adam Smith was sure that the free play of economic enterprise would be more beneficial than the intervention of the government in matters of commerce. Thomas Jefferson saw opportunities for endless progress if central governments could be reduced to the minimum. And scientists generally assumed that the free pursuit of scientific knowledge and its free exchange among all men would lead to perpetual progress and ultimately to universal peace.

Today, students of politics and economics have long since ceased to rely on such simple formulas as that that government is best which governs least and that the free play of the market will inevitably produce prosperity for everyone. The change may have come about because the political scientists and economists were not themselves the persons principally concerned; they had something of the detachment of the outside observer. But for the natural scientists the belief in the desirability of the complete freedom of science was much more than a hypothesis to be tested: it was a firm article of faith and a foundation for personal security. This general belief, in spite of individual incidents that seemed only to prove its validity, went almost unquestioned so far as any important public issue was concerned until World War II. And then all at once it began to seem evident to some parts of the public—in the way that such oversimplifications are usually taken as gospel—

that the safety of the United States depended on the American monopoly of the atomic bomb; that a great many scientists wanted to give it away out of motives of mistaken idealism, and others might be spies or traitors; and that all scientists ought therefore to be watched constantly by the F.B.I. or counterintelligence agencies. This shift, so far as its effect on individual scientists was concerned, was a little like bringing Thomas Jefferson to life and forcing him to subscribe to the New Deal programs for the support of farm prices, or resurrecting Nicholas Biddle and making him do business under the regulations of the Federal Reserve System and the Securities and Exchange Commission. It was even worse. It subjected scientists, whose professional attitude toward government was that of the late eighteenth century, not only to a changed set of public policies, but also to the most annoying and humiliating form of personal supervision.

In a way, however, the issues of loyalty and security only brought out more clearly a number of contradictions that had always existed. In the theory of science itself there was always a latent contradiction between the idea of a completely mechanical system of cause and effect on the one hand and, on the other, the idea of scientists as rational men with purposes and wills of their own. This contradiction perhaps caused the least trouble in the physical sciences. In those fields of knowledge the scientist could manage his thought in two compartments. In one he could think of his subject matter according to the strictest principles of cause and effect; in the other he could think of himself and his colleagues as the most independent of beings and could believe that their pursuit of knowledge and their freedom and financial support were essential to the progress of society. There is nothing less coldly scientific than a banquet speech at a scientific convention in which the speaker caitlinSecurity and Publicity Risks

discusses the nature of academic freedom or the role of science
and scientists in society.

It was this sort of contradiction that made it possible for
science to make its most dynamic contribution to society.
Whitehead has noted that the greatest invention of the nineteenth century was the invention of the method of invention
—the discovery by professional and scholarly groups of the way
in which the scientific profession could train its members, in-
duce them to contribute to the sum total of abstract knowledge,
and then organize its contribution to the advance of technology.[1] This development revolutionized the technology of industry and agriculture and, as we have seen, helped to make
basic changes in the nature of American government.

In all these matters science was anything but a detached
affair in an ivory tower. I do not mean science as only a method
of thought or as an organized body of knowledge, but science
as including also the organized groups of scientists. In this
sense science was a revolutionary force, and the physical sciences
most of all—and all the more so as they have increased, with
redoubled acceleration, the possibilities of man's control of
physical forces, from which naturally follow the possibilities
of control over other men.

On the other hand the social sciences, which seemed to a
great many people to be frighteningly radical in the days when
most social scientists were hardly to be distinguished from hu-
manists or philosophers or theologians, have been getting more
and more conservative in their social implications as they have
become more scientific. For the more scientific they become,
the more the scientists think of the social system as something
produced by a sequence of cause and effect that it would be

[1] Alfred N. Whitehead, *Science and the Modern World* (New York: The New
American Library, 1952), Chapter VI.

99

folly, if not impiety, to attempt to change. It was the mission-aries and their medical and agricultural colleagues who were determined to introduce technical assistance to underdeveloped countries with the purpose of revolutionizing them and their beliefs. But today many of the social scientists seem to be fright-ened by policies designed to upset the social structure or alter the cultures of other societies.

It is becoming less and less possible for even the physical scientist to ignore, or to expect society and government to ig-nore, the public consequences of his work. By inventing the method of invention he has telescoped the time from the dis-covery of a basic scientific fact to its technical development, and then on to its mass application. During the past half cen-tury it was hard for anyone to see what the development of the automobile was doing to the physical layout of our cities and to the nature of the social system. If some prophet could have foreseen those changes and could have condensed the next half-century's changes into a brief moving picture (as biologists sometimes show a year's growth of an organism in a short movie sequence), the American people might have been more frightened by this prospect in 1900 than they are today by the atomic bomb. If they had seen clearly what was coming, I wonder whether they would have reformed their city govern-ments and strengthened their city planning machinery more rapidly, or whether instead they would simply have lynched the first automotive engineers.

But in 1900 Americans were spared any knowledge of the social effects of the automobile, as we cannot be spared some idea of the possible consequences of the atomic bomb. Con-sequently we have to face up much more consciously to the issue whether to organize our governmental system more effectively to protect the freedom and integrity of science and to control the social application of its findings. The only practical alterna-

tive that I can imagine—one that I refuse to consider seriously
—is to lynch all the scientists.

The most difficult problems of maintaining the integrity of
science today come from the enforcement of the federal loyalty
and security programs, recently combined into a single security
program. But they are not the only problems of the kind. From
the point of view of science as such they may not even be the
most difficult to solve. Before we consider them, let us have a
look at some of the older types of problems that arise when
science and scientists become involved in political conflict and
their scientific integrity is challenged.

It is easy, of course, to recall cases in which the social sciences
became entangled in political disputes. For example, a few
years ago the Bureau of Agricultural Economics, in the Department of Agriculture, found its budget severely cut by the
Appropriations Committee of the House of Representatives.
The reason was that, in the eyes of some Congressmen, the
Bureau had gone beyond the business of scientific research and
had undertaken in addition to help the Secretary of Agriculture
plan his policies and program. In the eyes of other Congressmen, the Bureau had been much too coldly scientific and not
sufficiently earnest and aggressive in advocating policies to
benefit the farmers as compared with the general consuming
public.[2]

Or you can take a case from the history of the Bureau of
Labor Statistics. Its Cost-of-Living Index had been carefully
compiled for many years, and all interested statisticians knew
what costs were included in the Index and the limits on its
proper use. They understood that it represented the cost of a
number of staple commodities under certain conditions and
did not pretend to be a barometer of the total cost of living

---

[2] Charles M. Hardin, "The Bureau of Agricultural Economics Under Fire:
A Study in Valuation Conflicts," *Journal of Farm Economics*, XXVIII, No.
3 (August 1946), pp. 635-60.

under all conditions. But it became so useful that these limitations were forgotten. Corporations and labor unions began to make wages dependent on changes in the Index, and during the war those who enforced the regulations of wages also began to cite its data to support their actions.

When the government tried to hold wages down during the war it was not surprising that the labor unions resented the attempts and attacked the data on which the Index was based. They leveled their heaviest fire during 1943 and 1944 at the Bureau of Labor Statistics and its Index. It was only after review by a series of committees set up by the President, and after minor changes in the Index itself, that the attacks subsided and the Index regained its status as a generally accepted and nonpartisan set of figures.[3]

It is easy enough to say that these things happen because the social sciences are not scientific at all, that their subject matter is all mixed up with questions of values, and that when they deal with such values they therefore inevitably get into politics. This is a notion that comforts a great many physical and biological scientists, for it suggests that devotion to the natural sciences can keep you out of political trouble. It seems to me, however, that this idea is wrong in theory and useless in practice.

It seems so not because I think that the social sciences are now able, or will ever be able, to use the same method as the natural sciences. On the contrary, I suspect that they can do themselves a great deal of harm by trying to apply methods that do not fit their subject matter. As a layman I am prepared to believe with Dr. Conant that each "universe of inquiry" has a different method that is most appropriate to its problems.[4]

[3] Harold Stein, Editor, *Public Administration and Policy Development* (New York: Harcourt, Brace and Company, 1952), pp. 775-853.

[4] James B. Conant, *Modern Science and Modern Man* (New York: Columbia University Press, 1952), pp. 99-100.

Nevertheless, that is not the point. The real point, it seems to me, is that the political trouble comes in the phase where scientific findings are being applied to practical problems, and in this phase the natural sciences are just as deeply involved and just as vulnerable to political attack as the social sciences.

The economists and statisticians at the Bureau of Agricultural Economics and the Bureau of Labor Statistics, in the cases I have cited, were pretty clear in their own understanding of what facts could be established by objective research and what had to be decided as a policy or political issue. The trouble was not that they as scientists were unable to draw this distinction, but that their political superiors and their political opponents were not willing to respect the distinction or to let them do so.

It is easy enough to think of cases in which equally violent political attacks were directed at natural scientists. As recently as 1953 the Director of the National Bureau of Standards, Dr. Astin, was about to be dismissed by his political superior, the Secretary of Commerce, because his scientists had found that a certain chemical preparation was of practically no value in prolonging the useful life of automobile batteries. This finding had led the Post Office Department to forbid the advertising of the battery additive through the mails, and the Secretary of Commerce considered this an unwarranted interference with private enterprise.

Then you may recall the famous case of oleomargarine in Iowa, a case that involved both the natural and the social sciences. A few years ago the dairy interests demanded that a young research assistant at Iowa State College be dismissed for publishing a study in which he found that margarine was as nutritious as butter and a more efficient means of producing edible fats during wartime shortages. And if you are interested not merely in the bread-and-butter issues of our economic system, but also in the more elevated issues of the origin and destiny of man, you may even remember the comic case of Mr. Scopes, who was prosecuted during the twenties in Tennessee for using *The Origin of Species* rather than the Book of Genesis as a text for his high-school science class.

In cases like these the real issues went far beyond the question of the freedom of science in any narrow sense. The question was not whether the scientist should be free to conduct research and exchange objective ideas with his fellow scientists. It was how this freedom affected public policy. In each of the cases I have mentioned the scientists came off very well indeed. Mr. Scopes became famous in the process of discrediting the Tennessee state legislature and destroying its effort to restrict the teaching of evolution. The scientist at Iowa went elsewhere and got a better job, after having helped to discredit the butter lobby, which later lost out completely in its effort to maintain restrictions on the marketing of margarine. And Dr. Astin was reinstated in his job with the full confidence, so it was said, of the Secretary of Commerce, a happy ending that came about partly on the scientific merits of the case, partly because organized science was able to marshal a large body of influential support in a most effective political protest, and partly because the Secretary of Commerce apparently learned a great deal from the incident and was big enough to admit it.

In each of these cases the crucial question was really outside the scope of scientific research. It was whether an oversimplified and conventional scientific theory should be taught in the public schools in place of an oversimplified version of a religious dogma. Or it was the issue whether, from virtually unquestioned scientific facts, reports ought to be issued that would favor a product in competition with that of a local industry. Or it was whether, given an apparent disagreement among experts, governmental regulatory agencies should seek to have the issue determined by more thorough tests or should let consumers find out for themselves whether a product was useful. In each of these cases, in short, it seems to me that the scientists who in general rushed to the defense of their colleague were really defending his right to supply data to the public or to public officials on problems not altogether within the scope of his research. And I think that in each case the scientists were right.

Those who choose to make a political attack on any particular policy are always glad to avoid the necessity of attacking the policy head on, especially if it has substantial public support. It is sometimes much easier and just as effective to leave the policy in effect but to cripple its administration. This is an old tactic with respect to local laws on gambling and morals, but it has been used too on issues of national economic policy. Another tactic, more to our purpose, is to attack the scientific or research foundations on which the policy is based. It might distress the public to admit that you are quite willing to have the Post Office carry advertisements for a product that is chemically worthless; it is much easier to argue that the government scientists that have tested the product are personally prejudiced or unsympathetic to the ideal of a free market. You never repeal laws against gambling or openly attack the judge for sentencing gamblers; it is just as effective to intimidate the policemen who report the existence of a bookie or a roulette wheel.

Issues like these suggest that in American political controversy the scientific agency is the one likely to come first under attack. No issue can be rationally discussed unless the contesting parties either come to a willing agreement on the basic facts or accept the ruling of a higher authority. And in American political life there has been much more of a disposition for each party to hire its own experts than to agree readily with any paramount authority.

In these circumstances science needs to build defenses for its integrity on two levels. First of all it needs to defend the integrity of science itself. To do so requires freedom of thought and of publication for basic research. These freedoms in turn can be protected only if fundamental science is sustained by a great many strong and independent institutions drawing their financial support from a wide variety of sources. This end I am confident we can accomplish in America, since we have invented ways of protecting the independence even of those institutions that are supported by governmental funds.

But the second level of defense is a more difficult problem. This is the level of the application of science to practical problems. Here, too, science must be protected. For it is of no use to imagine that you can defend pure science alone. Our history has committed us too deeply to the habit of mixing basic research with practical and applied research and of encouraging scientists and engineers to move into positions with executive and administrative responsibility. If we cannot defend the integrity of science in its application to public affairs, we shall not be able to maintain support for basic science and defend its right to freedom of inquiry.

Science, in short, cannot exist on the basis of a treaty of strict nonaggression with the rest of society; from either side, there is no defensible frontier. We can, and must, maintain strong and independent universities and research institutions and insist on their right of freedom of research. But we cannot insist on their freedom on the argument that they are engaged only in basic science, which does not interfere with public affairs or bear on controversial issues. This has not been a useful argument since the scientists came out of the monasteries, and since we give up the ideal of separating society into distinct "estates," with all those who could read and write claiming the privileges of the clergy. Our argument for the freedom of science must rest instead on the conviction that such freedom is justified both by the importance of freedom for its own sake, as the fundamental value in political society, and by the historical evidence that only free science can play a dynamic role in furthering human welfare. The scientists of Germany, who thought that science was so separate from politics that it could prosper no matter what political philosophy dominated the government, discovered their mistake under Hitler.

On the other hand, we are not likely to favor a system in which some science, or some body of scientists, would have full control over the application of science to public affairs. The various branches of science themselves are not very likely, as a matter of theory, to accept the domination of any single school of thought. It is hard to find any scientists in this country who believe that the materialist dialectic, for example, can provide all the answers to our political problems. The few who were tempted by this aberration a decade or two ago have been cured by the Lysenko case and by the whole history of Communist experience that it typifies.[5]

The problem, then, is to devise a political system by which the freedom of research can be defended and its results applied to practical problems under the guidance of responsible democratic processes.

Here we must distinguish very carefully between an unchecked and doctrinaire system of central authority on the one hand, and a responsible system of central administration on the other. The typical scientist is so strongly opposed to arbitrary authority that he is impatient with any type of central administration. Yet it seems to me that the political attacks on the integrity of science are—in the United States—more often

[5] Conway Zirkle, "The Involuntary Destruction of Science in the USSR," *Scientific Monthly*, LXXVI, No. 5 (May 1953), pp. 277-83.

the result of the weakness or absence of central administration than they are of its having too much authority.

The general public cannot be expected to understand the technical issues involved in any dispute over the objectivity and accuracy of any particular research program. Even the most sophisticated members of the public cannot be expected to take time to interest themselves in such disputes. It is for this reason that, as we have noted, each of the opposing sides in any political controversy is always tempted to attack the scientists who produce data and recommendations adverse to its interests. Such attacks can come, of course, from any direction—from those inside the government as well as from private citizens, from career administrators or military officers as well as from investigating Congressmen. But generally, it seems to me, the attacks come most frequently from irresponsible special interests, and least frequently from those whose general responsibilities make them aware of the need for objective and unbiased research.

I have discussed the strengths of the American government that have come from the high degree of independence with which its scientific careers have developed and its specialized bureaus grown up. But this system has the defects of its virtues. It must be admitted that the high degree of specialization in the government structure and the public careers of the United States has been connected with (and perhaps has helped to cause) a considerable weakness in central administration. And the unhappy result, from the point of view of science, has been twofold: first, in the conduct of public affairs, the scientist is tempted to push into controversial areas where he is vulnerable to attack, simply because no one else is competent to do the job; second, when he is then under fire there is no one else competent to take the responsibility and to defend him.

There needs to be, in short, an intervening layer of administration between science and politics, to protect science and to make their relationship more smooth. The lack of this layer has been as much responsible as any personal malevolence for the political attacks that have been made on the integrity of science.

It is in this context, it seems to me, that we ought to look at the federal loyalty and security program as it affects science. The problem is more often considered as a problem of individual rights or personal justice and analyzed in terms of human freedom or equitable procedure. These, I agree, are the main aspects of the loyalty and security problem in general. But I am not going to deal mainly with these aspects, partly because others have done so more fully and competently than I could hope to do,[6] and partly because these aspects are not peculiar to the relationship of science to government.

Someone has remarked that the martyrdom of scientists is often overrated. Galileo suffered nothing worse than a mild protective custody, whereas Savonarola was hanged and Servetus was burned at the stake. Similarly, in what is sometimes called the Washington witch-hunt, the scientists have probably fared better than others, in spite of the fact that much of the public hysteria has been generated by the idea of the loss of our atomic secrets. The public prestige of the scientific professions, the strong feeling of community among the scientists, and the practical motive of not wasting human assets that might help in the production of new weapons—these factors have weighed in the balance to protect scientists more than others. Few who know the Washington scene would doubt that the Department of Defense and the Atomic Energy Commission, which employ or support the great majority of the scientists, have had far less

---

6 See Eleanor Bontecou, *The Federal Loyalty-Security Program* (Ithaca: Cornell University Press, 1953), and Walter Gellhorn, *Security, Loyalty, and Science* (Ithaca: Cornell University Press, 1950).

trouble from Congressional attacks, and have administered their security programs with far more equity and competence, than has the Department of State.

Let me start with the stubborn view that I refuse to accept the dilemma between national security and individual freedom. I believe that our national government exists primarily to protect individual liberties and not to restrict them, and I think the doctrine that the end justifies the means very dangerous medicine for a political system. On the other hand, I am afraid there is no question that those scholars and scientists who talked of the problem of secrecy as if spies did not exist, and as if counterintelligence measures were unnecessary, were not aware of the kind of world they have the misfortune to live in.

No one can calculate the damage to our national morale that has been inflicted by those who have made political capital out of reckless charges against public officials in general and scientists in particular.[7] But, again on the other hand, much of the practical difficulty in the enforcement of the security system in our defense research programs has come from the fact that the scientists best able to exercise discriminating judgment on matters of secrecy and security were by temperament and tradition so impatient with the idea that they left this business too much to people who knew too little about it. A very great deal of trouble has come, not from any fundamental conflict

---

7 "Under the plea that the structure of American society is in imminent peril of being shattered by a satanic conspiracy, dangerous developments are taking place today in our national life. Favored by an atmosphere of intense disquiet and suspicion, a subtle but potent assault upon basic human rights is now in progress. Some Congressional inquiries have revealed a distinct tendency to become inquisitions. These inquisitions, which find their historic pattern in medieval Spain and in the tribunals of modern totalitarian states, begin to constitute a threat to freedom of thought in this country." From the text of the letter issued by the General Council of the Presbyterian Church in the U.S.A. to its congregations, as published in *The New York Times*, November 3, 1953.

between scientific freedom on the one hand and security considerations on the other, but from political irresponsibility and sheer incompetence.

The primary judgment in the security program, of course, is what you are going to choose to keep secret. This, it cannot be said too often, is not something to decide automatically on the basis merely of judging what a potential enemy would like to know and then trying to keep him from knowing it. Let me give a simple analogy. If the ordinary tourist's maps of the major American cities were not given away at every filling station, and if no similar maps had ever been manufactured, it would be worth a great deal of money to an enemy nation to have them prepared. Nevertheless, the layman can see quite readily that it would not be worth while to keep such maps a secret from the strategic bombing forces of all other countries. It would simply be too much of a nuisance to the American public; moreover, it would cost too much in terms of the handicap it would place on the normal working of our society. Any layman can see this point, but no layman, without making a very special effort, can judge sensibly whether a certain scientific discovery or bit of research data should be kept a secret. For he is likely to be overimpressed by the mystery of science and bemused by the hope that other scientists will not be able to do what our scientists have done. This self-delusion makes him want to keep things secret that it is hopeless to conceal for any length of time. And similarly he has little reason to appreciate the handicaps that secrecy places on our own scientific progress. It is all very well in a cross-country race to hide the road maps to deceive your competitor, but it is something of a nuisance if by doing so you send all your own drivers down blind alleys.

For this reason it is possible to make a sensible decision on what should or should not be kept secret only if a responsible administrative system, in an atmosphere free from political pressure and emotion, considers each question with the most balanced judgment possible.

An administrative system of this kind can be properly balanced only if it brings to bear the special knowledge of the trained intelligence agent, who knows something about the purposes and techniques of espionage, and the special knowledge of the scientist, who knows something about the subject matter under consideration. In setting up such a system it is desirable to get a proper balance. But it is essential to get something that will work, and it may not be possible to wait for perfection. And I suppose it has never been possible to imagine that you could ever set up a security or intelligence system to make the routine decisions on what should be released and what should be kept secret, if you had to wait until you staff it with research scientists. Moreover, it is in the last analysis fairly safe to say that any officer in command in the military departments would hardly be enthusiastic about turning such decisions over to scientists. I know, of course, that the security classification of each item is normally determined by the individual worker, and thus that scientists make such determinations. But they generally do so within the limits of policies determined by military and security officers, and certainly the basic questions on what information should be released to other nations is firmly kept within the control of military officers whose main concern and training is with the intelligence program. At the highest level this situation is reflected in the fact that intelligence is the most important military function not covered for the Secretary of Defense by an assistant secretary or by a substantial civilian staff in his own office.

But whatever distortion this arrangement may introduce, I cannot propose an alternative that would be practicable tomorrow. And in any case this distortion is a minor one compared with that caused by the fear of Congressional investigation. Everyone dealing with security affairs has an overwhelming motive to play it safe, to run no personal risks, and to give each item a high enough security classification so that he can never be criticized by his political superiors. On important issues this motive goes much deeper. It would be dangerous to propose an action that might seem to a Congressman or a Congressional staff investigator to indicate an undesirable degree of sympathy with foreign nations or a willingness to part with our precious secrets.

It is important to emphasize that I am not talking about a general policy of the Congress. Still less am I talking about a law enacted by the Congress. I am talking about a tendency that is particularly dangerous because it is one of the few things in the American government that the Congress cannot control at all. For the one thing in the United States that the Congress will never call into question is whatever is done by one of its own committees.

This political irresponsibility in the basic structure of the Congress is not something required by the Constitution. Each House has full authority to create committees, or not to create them, and to prescribe the conditions under which they are to work. But in practice each House grants to its committees —to special investigating committees and their staff members as well as to legislative and appropriations committees—more arbitrary discretion than is permitted to any other part of our governmental structure.

Our inferior courts are subject to review by the Supreme Court, which is bound by legal precedent and the criticism of a vigilant community of lawyers. Our executive agencies are subject to discipline by the President, to rigorous supervision by Congressional committees, and to review by the courts. But

Congressional committees are effectively responsible to nobody; indeed, the chairman of a Congressional committee is hardly responsible even to the committee itself.

On most of the ordinary policy issues the leaders of Congressional committees are restrained by their sense of personal responsibility, by the views of their party leaders, and by the influence of their colleagues. But the issues of loyalty and security are so explosive and offer such tremendous temptations in the form of free advertising and political power that the traditional restraints of the Congressional system have been simply ineffective.

The difficulty with the security program is that its basic outlines have been influenced too greatly by fright and prejudice and too little by hard common sense. It is instructive to recall by way of comparison the episode of the Eighteenth Amendment. Here, too, was a case in which a popular moral fervor was used by cynical politicians to put into effect an unworkable general law. The amateur enthusiast is always tempted to adopt absolute views. It is the professional administrator who contributes a certain amount of critical and practical realism to make these sweeping views workable. In a matter like prohibition the difficulties were overcome, until repeal, only by a kind of mass national hypocrisy. This did a great deal of harm, but it did not involve the basic security of the nation. Our emotional approach in recent years toward the loyalty and security program seems to me much more dangerous. It is dangerous because it applies an abstract rule in an impractical way, without taking the practical and discriminating measures necessary to accomplish the proper purpose.

First of all there is the business of making a great to-do over the loyalty and security of government workers, and perhaps of teachers, and ignoring everybody else. To anyone concerned with the national defense it must seem ridiculous to spend a great deal of time and effort investigating the background of a clerk in the General Accounting Office, or an accountant in the Veterans' Administration, or a technician in the Fish and Wildlife Service, while ignoring the employees of airlines and radio stations and railroads and private power plants. It is a similar lack of discrimination and common sense that leads to the wholesale denial of passports and visas to scientists who wish to attend international meetings. This practice makes it nearly impossible to have certain types of scientific gatherings in the United States at all, and it humiliates America all over the world in the eyes of scientists who believe in freedom.

Next, the loyalty program, as a separate program, was always fundamentally impractical. It was impractical because its basic criteria were so vague that they were almost impossible to define, and even when defined they were likely to catch only past offenders. It set a great number of civil service investigators, many of whom would have been entirely competent to check up on credit ratings or traffic violations, inquiring into the finest sort of distinctions in political philosophy and filling the files in Washington with meaningless gossip. And finally, the only penalty that it provided—discharge for disloyalty—was so heavy that it was difficult to use against anyone not virtually an active traitor. It the eighteenth century, you will recall, when juries were called on to inflict the death sentence for petty theft they simply found people not guilty, and a reduction in the severity of the criminal code brought about much more effective law enforcement.

It seems to me, therefore, that two of the most recent changes in the loyalty and security system are all to the good: first, those that let each department decide which posts are sensitive ones and which are not; secondly, those that merge the loyalty and security programs together in a single security effort.

Next, it seems to me clear from our history that the combination of a career judiciary and a career police service has always proved much less a danger to personal liberty than a system of vigilantes. I share the regret of many of the critics of the security system that it has been necessary to institute in American life a system of police files on individual citizens. It is obvious that this opens the door to grave abuses—to the leaks of unsubstantiated gossip to blackmailers, to the destruction of personal reputations, and to the beginnings of political persecution. (The surest way to destroy the security system itself is to begin to give the impression that it is going to be used to help Democrats win elections over Republicans, or vice versa.) Yet espionage and subversion are painful facts, and I see no way to deal with them by any other means than by a federal enforcement system, including a federal police agency.

I am inclined to suspect that some of the greatest difficulties in the security system have come when those in high official positions have disliked the security function and left it to the special security officers or to committees of subordinates. The enforcement of security regulations, especially those involved in the consideration of appointments and removals, is a painful and disagreeable business. Yet it seems to me that anyone who disapproves of lynchings has to be ready to serve on a jury. If the top responsible officers are willing to give their time and attention to the security problem, they will probably find that it costs them less time in the long run, and that they can make tremendous savings in the morale of their staff and in their relationships with the scientific community. This seems to me the only way to bring the security business into the main stream of executive responsibility, which is exactly where it belongs.

The responsible executive is likely to be a better judge of the security of an immediate subordinate than anyone else. An investigating agent is bound to develop a professional bias.

He is hired to be suspicious. In collecting information he is likely, even with the best of training, to bring in a great deal of unrelated gossip from the next-door neighbor, the filling station operator, and the disgruntled subordinate. For this there is no better balance than to get opinions on the man in question directly from his professional colleagues and his immediate superiors. There is a great deal of practical wisdom in the ancient maxim that a man deserves trial by a jury of his peers. It is only his own equals and associates—responsible men in a similar line of business—who are intellectually capable of evaluating his ideas, his character, and his efficiency. If a federal executive is willing to take the trouble to gather such evidence and make up his own mind, he is considerably less likely to do injustice in the administration of the security program.

The Federal Bureau of Investigation, along with its tremendous general popularity and acclaim, has come in for a certain amount of criticism from political liberals. I think, however, that its critics should take a couple of things into account. The first is that the Director of the F.B.I., by contrast with some of his enthusiastic supporters in the Congress, has always tried to avoid having the F.B.I. made responsible for evaluating the information it collects, or for making decisions in individual cases. The second is that the F.B.I., simply because it has had high standards in the recruitment of its staff, has done a more discriminating and intelligent job than the investigating staffs of several other federal agencies. It has had the merit of a comparatively disciplined career system. The abuses of its materials have come from the fact that it has not been enough of a career system; I suspect that some former agents of the F.B.I., working for Congressional committees and private groups, have been responsible for greater danger to personal privacy and individual reputations than have any of the official agencies.

For similar reasons the military departments have probably dealt in a more fair and responsible manner with the security problem than have most of the civilian departments. Some of the unfairness in decisions on individual cases, I suspect, has come from the personal fear and insecurity of the adjudicating officials. The executive or the members of the reviewing committee are likely to be afraid to judge a case on its merits lest it become the object of the attentions of a Congressional committee. They are likely to look on an employee under investigation, not as a potential security risk, but as a certain publicity risk. This fear is particularly likely to affect the person whose own status and position are somewhat in doubt.

This kind of worry can lead appointing authorities to deprive the government of a large share of the potential supply of talent. The appointing officer is not willing to choose the best candidate who may be judged to be loyal and trustworthy; he begins to shy away from anyone about whom the more zealous security officers may entertain a suspicion, for he is unwilling to run the risk that the security officers may begin to suspect him for his sympathy with suspicious characters. Even if the appointing officer is immune to such fears, however, he cannot ignore a consideration that leads him to the same course of action. If he wants to get on with an important job, he is going to search for candidates who have already received their security clearance or who are sure to be cleared without delays or question. The effect of this motive is the same as the effect of personal cowardice: it operates to deprive the government of a large proportion of potentially valuable public servants. And the available supply is not large enough to make us want to waste it.

During my own brief period of responsibility it seemed to me that the regular officers of the military services were likely to be less vulnerable to such fears, and therefore more able to exercise objective and discriminating judgment, than many of their civilian colleagues. Their attitude in such matters can be thoroughly professional. They are likely to have no sympathy whatever for the idealistic view of the scientist who a few years ago was inclined to believe in "One World" and in the ready sharing of all scientific information. On the other hand, they are likely to look on such ideas as no more shocking than many of the other odd ideas that civilians are likely to hold, and therefore as not worth punishment. And the regular military officer is most likely to be immune to the temptation to believe that anyone who was in favor of our alliance with the Russians during World War II is by that fact subversive; it is easy for him to remember that alliances change, and that high-ranking generals were exchanging decorations for themselves and their staffs along the Elbe in the summer of 1945.

Thomas Jefferson argued that it would be easier to preserve freedom in a large federated republic than in a small city-state, because the passions of local prejudice would cancel each other out within a great federal system. It seems to me that something like this has been true of the security programs. The executive branch has been far more centralized than the legislative branch, and therefore has attained a far more judicious balance between considerations of secrecy on the one hand and, on the other hand, considerations of justice and of the efficiency of the government. And the federal Congress, even though it has permitted several committees to operate in this field with widely different standards of policy, has been greatly surpassed in irresponsibility by the similar committees set up by a number of the state legislatures. The security review machinery in a federal department may sometimes do an injustice if it dismisses an employee for belonging to an organization on the Attorney General's list. But it would make ten times as many mistakes if it took as equally authoritative the citations of Congressional committees, and a hundred times as many if it relied on the lists of organizations and individuals who have been cited by the various investigating committees in state legislatures.

Much the same thing is true in the protection of scientists against political attacks on their objectivity. Several of the most discriminating students of federal and state research programs have noted that the federal system of grants-in-aid, coupled with the limited degree of federal supervision of the state agencies, has protected the scientists in state agencies from attacks on their scientific integrity for local political purposes.

It is interesting to speculate on the comparative political attitudes of scientists of various denominations. If it were possible to take some sort of Gallup poll on the political opinions of scientists and people in related professional fields, I suspect that it would show that the mathematicians and physicists have tended to be the most radical, the chemists rather conservative, and the doctors the most conservative of all. If there is any truth in this idea, I suspect it is because the physicists have been more convinced than any other scientists that their science possesses the key to the riddle of the universe, and they see no reason why, by bold and speculative thinking, the practical problems of politics could not be solved overnight. The chemists, by contrast, are much more accustomed to teamwork with engineers and administrators in relatively stable industries; they are much more aware that the abstract sciences do not always lead directly to practical application; and they are much less ready to extend their own field of knowledge and its techniques to provide the guidelines for what Dr. Conant calls the other "universes of inquiry." And the doctors, of course, are trained by every hour of their experience to see how hard and slow a job it is to apply the results of science to the affairs of human beings.

This is all sheer speculation, based on the most unscientific kind of personal observation. And even if it is true, it is significant only with respect to speculative thought. For when it comes to the issues of loyalty and security, the physicists are as practical and moralistic as any in making judgments about the loyalty and security of their colleagues. The Congressional investigator and the security officer apply a kind of parody of a scientific method when they are the most unfair. As a matter of statistical probability I suppose it may be true that you could find a larger proportion of subversives among the foreign-born or their children than in the families of those who have been American citizens for several generations. It is also probable, I suppose, that there are more communists among those who voted the Labor Party ticket in New York than among those who voted the Republican ticket in North Dakota. But on such issues the physicist who works for the government knows better than to try to apply any such perversion of a scientific method; he does not want to be considered as an impersonal unit in any system of statistical probability. He wants justice on the basis of a discriminating judgment regarding his quality as a unique individual, as a free citizen, and as a morally responsible being. And he is absolutely right.

Some day, perhaps, we shall have the benefit of a comprehensive philosophy that will harmonize the newest theories of the most advanced sciences with the moral principles imbedded in our tradition of the common law and in the safeguards of our constitutional system. For the present the way of thinking of the scientist and the way of thinking of the lawyer or philosopher who believes that the principles of morality and justice are not merely relative, are in a most uneasy theoretical relationship. But we may be wiser in our practice than in our abstract philosophy. We have to build the administrative institutions that will both make use of science and guarantee freedom and justice to scientists. These same institutions must weld the various scientific programs into a single whole, into a practical unity more coherent than any of our present systems of philosophy. Perhaps our action must precede our metaphysics; and this practical effort may some day contribute to the development of the harmonizing philosophy itself.

In the government of Great Britain the mystique of monarchy has been the force around which authority has united for more than a millennium. Under the shelter of this unifying idea developed His Majesty's government and His Majesty's civil service, and the supposedly omnipotent Parliament has never permitted its own members or committees to interfere with the majestic unity of that system. Similarly, under the shelter of the Cabinet's authority the University Grants Committee makes public funds available for academic and research purposes, leaving absolute freedom to the universities for the conduct of their research. And similarly, with the benefit of royal patronage, the Royal Society continues to be the sponsor of science in the twentieth century, as it was in the seventeenth.

In the United States we have not done nearly so well in building up freedom under the shelter of strong central authority. It is easy enough to see that our freedom is more threatened by the elements of irresponsibility within our system than by any strong central executive; indeed, it seems probable that our freedom would be furthered in general, and particularly that the objectivity and integrity of government research would be best protected, by a more authoritative and responsible executive supported by a strong and stable career service.

In only one field has popular support made this combination

even halfway possible in the United States. Nowhere in our civilian government have Americans supported the creation of strong and stable administrative institutions and protected them from capricious political persecution. Our military tradition, however, is a quite different matter. Within the military services there is a tradition of permanence and of discipline that enables the military services to be entrusted with a necessary degree of discretion, stability, and secrecy in the conduct of the public's business. If we really wish to defend the integrity of science in America and to maintain the supremacy of civilian political authority, we might do well to build up a similarly strong administrative service and career system on the civilian side of the federal government.

Natural scientists used to believe that their research work, unlike that of the social scientists, was clearly enough apart from the controversial issues of politics to enable them to defend their integrity in isolation. This position is getting harder and harder to defend. It is desirable, indeed, to distinguish as clearly as possible between those things that science can prove and those that have to be decided by debate and an appeal to the ultimate political authority, the electorate. This distinction will make it possible to give the working scientist the freedom to do objective research and to publish it among his colleagues. But this distinction is not an automatic one. It can be maintained only by a stable and competent executive, responsible to the people through orderly political processes. To make the United States government more competent and responsible is the most likely way to assure the freedom and integrity of science in the America of the future.

V

THE

MACHINERY OF ADVICE

In public and private administration alike it is becoming the fashion to rely less on the direct line of executive authority and more on persuasion and agreement through various types of committee procedures and advisory machinery. Policy is no longer made by the inspired amateur in parliamentary discussions, nor administrative decisions by the executive who always acts quickly and is sometimes right.

This trend in managerial fashion is welcomed by some who see in it a new manifestation of democracy in administration. It is looked on with contempt by a hardy few who follow Charles G. Dawes in thinking that the appointment of an advisory committee is the last refuge of administrative incompetence. Regardless of this difference of opinion, the increase in the use of advisory machinery is probably an inevitable result of the growing complexity of public affairs and of the need to make major decisions in the light of the most objective and expert knowledge available. Such machinery has been set up in its most elaborate fashion in the government's scientific programs.

How do you organize to get the kind of scientific advice you need from outside the government? The first answer to this question has usually been to create more or less formal advisory committees, made up partly or wholly of experts from private institutions.

The standing advisory committee is certainly a familiar administrative device; it has been used for many years in all the scientific programs of the government. Most of these committees have been set up only by action of the executive agency concerned, but a few have been dignified by statutory status, and two or three have been given functions that almost amount to the exercise of executive authority.

The most elaborate structure of advisory committees has undoubtedly been erected by the agencies that have developed the contractual system in its most extensive form, the Atomic Energy Commission and the Department of Defense.

In the Atomic Energy Commission, for example, the General Advisory Committee is looked on as the official spokesman for the scientists and engineers in advising the Commission. This Committee has not only statutory status, but also full access to secret information, the privilege of meeting regularly with the Commission, and a small office and staff in the Commission's headquarters. In addition the Commission has itself created more than a dozen part-time advisory committees to deal with various special aspects of its work.

The Department of Defense, partly for the purpose of helping to unify the military programs, created an even more extensive system of committees and geared it even more closely with the exercise of executive authority. Under the Research and Development Board, which was until 1953 the principal agent of the Secretary of Defense for the co-ordination of the scientific programs of the military services, about fifteen committees were established. Through them (and their subordinate panels) the Secretary of Defense attempted to review and supervise the military research programs, which included thousands of projects and spent in 1953 close to a billion and a half dollars.

At an even higher level in the executive structure a Science

Advisory Committee was created in the Office of Defense Mobilization in the Executive Office of the President. This Committee was made up entirely of eminent scientists from private life, who were to advise the O.D.M. and the President on the scientific aspects of mobilization and defense problems.

Part-time committees, however, are not the only type of advisory machinery. Particularly in the great programs of research for military purposes, two new types have been developed. One is the system of operations research. The other is the special study contract.

Operations research has been defined as the application of the scientific method to the study of the operations of large complex organizations or activities. It had earlier civilian uses, but its large-scale military use began when the scientists who had developed radar were asked how it ought to be used. In the Battle of Britain there was no time to wait to develop military doctrine by trial and error. The commanding officers had no margin of safety; they needed to know where antennas should be located and how signals could be interpreted, and scientists responded with precise mathematical and physical studies that doubled the effectiveness of the air defense system. Churchill was speaking of the Spitfire pilots, but he might well have meant the operations research men, when he said that seldom have so many owed so much to so few.

The simplest use of operations research was at the level of the use of weapons and equipment. One brief study, for example, showed that a small change in the detonation depth of a depth bomb made it five times as effective. Similar techniques were then used to make tactical decisions—for example, how high a bomber should fly, and in what kind of formation, and how much of its load should be devoted to bombs, to fuel, and to search instruments. Studies of this kind then became the foundation for more elaborate studies of two broader kinds.

First, operations research on tactical problems led to studies that were nearly broad enough to be called strategic. For example, operations research work showed how best to design the patterns of the patrol operations by which the German submarines were defeated in the Bay of Biscay. Next, it helped to show how the weapons and combinations of weapons should be developed into new systems; the study of weapons systems, by comparison with the strategic and tactical needs of the future, thus becomes the basis for planning the program of research and for the development of new weapons and new techniques.

Operations researchers, after their conspicuous wartime success, began looking for new worlds to conquer. In the United States they set up a special committee within the National Research Council and founded a new professional society. They publicized their military accomplishments as much as the rules of secrecy allowed, and they began to identify broader opportunities for their work in industry, and even to speculate on its use in the civilian branches of government. All this led to some jurisdictional rivalries; the management engineers were inclined to argue that they had been doing similar work for decades, and biological and social scientists of several denominations sometimes protested the dominant role of the physicists and mathematicians in the new guild. The social scientists could point to some considerable wartime accomplishments of their own, as in the work of the Information and Education Branch of the Army, which developed the "point system" for the release of soldiers at the end of the war, and in the studies of various sociologists and anthropologists on problems of psychological warfare.

But these were only the normal differences of outlook among specialists, and the operations research business, amalgamated with some related work in the social sciences, flourished in the immediate postwar years. All three military services, while carrying on some such research directly within their own organizations, made even greater use of the contractual system for its support. The Air Force, with the help of Douglas Aircraft and the Ford Foundation, created the Rand Corporation, with headquarters in Santa Monica, California. The Army undertook to support the Operations Research Office, a subsidiary of Johns Hopkins in the outskirts of Washington, and the Human Resources Research Office, on the George Washington University campus. The Navy made a contractual arrangement with the Massachusetts Institute of Technology, but played its cards a little closer to its chest: the Operations Evaluation Group, although its staff members were on the M.I.T. payroll, was set up physically in the office of the Chief of Naval Operations.

Finally, the techniques of the advisory committee and of operations research fused into a third method of providing independent advice: the special study contract. Such studies, in a sense, are extensions of the familiar type of *ad hoc* commission that is often set up to make a report to a public agency. But they add a new dimension to the old type of special commission; they bring together in elaborate organizations the resources of the natural sciences, along with the skills of the social sciences and policy judgment. And they often develop ideas that then become the basis for even larger engineering projects to develop those ideas in the form of new weapons systems. Thus, for example, Project Charles was a study of the problem of air defense, which was then followed by Project Lincoln (also at M.I.T. under Air Force contract), which was not only to study scientific possibilities, but also to develop the actual gadgets for practical use.[1]

---

1 Omar N. Bradley, "A Soldier's Farewell," *Saturday Evening Post*, August 29, 1953, p. 48.

The Machinery of Advice

By 1952 the military departments had set up so many studies of this kind and were competing so strenuously for the services of scientists and universities that the Research and Development Board insisted that they would have to get its approval before starting any new ones.

Yet, with all this apparatus, many leading scientists are dissatisfied with the way in which scientific advice is applied to the major problems of defense policy. Such dissatisfaction obviously does not come from any shortage in the quantity of advisory apparatus. It develops rather because scientists and executives are generally likely to think in quite different ways about the terms on which advice is offered and received.

The problem of advisory machinery would be quite simple if we could rely on the classical administrative theory that "the expert should be on tap but not on top"—which implies the availability of an anonymous or at least unobtrusive adviser whose expertise is at hand for the responsible executive to accept or not, in his own discretion. This theory might suit the executive well enough, but might not please the scientist, who is (with some reason) never happy to leave his advice entirely at the mercy of the administrator. In any case, it is a theory that applies to advisory machinery only when it has been established because the man inside the government wants advice from outside the government.

But this is only one of several possible reasons, and in practice not always the most important, for the creation of advisory machinery. Another is that men outside the government want influence over what is done inside the government. And a third reason is that the insider wants support as well as advice (or instead of advice) from the outsider. These several motives are usually mixed in various proportions, depending on the mixture of scientific and political considerations involved.

The difficulties in the use of advisory committees, it is probably fair to say, come less from the sins of the advisers than from the weakness of those who are getting the advice. An executive supported by a strong staff of career administrators (some of whom are trained as scientists) will be able to use the advice of all outside experts with discretion, especially if he is untroubled by political pressure or criticism. But this is not the world in which the American public official lives. He has to put together a staff on salary scales that cannot possibly attract, in competition with private industry, administrators or engineers of the highest order of ability. Those whom he can attract are usually induced to come for short-term assignments. To compensate for the weaknesses of his organization, and especially to bolster his standing with Congressional committees, he sets up committees of eminent experts, both to help him make decisions and to give prestige and support to the decisions he has already made. In less invidious terms, the advisory machinery constitutes the system by which the official keeps his professional counterparts in private life informed of his activities and more or less ready to be drafted for service in case of emergency.

The habit of leaning on advisory committees causes the least trouble in matters in which the executive wishes virtually to delegate certain types of decisions. For example, the National Science Foundation very properly arranges to have the National Research Council help it select the individuals to receive scientific fellowships. Such dependence causes relatively little trouble where the subject matter is highly specialized, with little apparent impact on practical affairs, as in decisions on basic research programs.

The trouble comes, however, where the problems considered by the advisory committee cut across difficult and controversial policies or affect influential private interests. In such situations there are some occasional difficulties about making use of the scientist as adviser—difficulties that are the fault of the scientist himself. Being human as well as a specialist, he is tempted, and sometimes takes delight in yielding to the temptation, to ignore things outside his special competence, to believe that there is no need for responsible authority, and to assume that his scientific approach is undiluted by personal bias.

I shall always remember with particular pleasure the medical research doctor in one of the military departments who assured a Catholic chaplain that the problem of birth control was one that was purely scientific and thus by definition one with which the chaplain had no concern. I thought at first that he was making this argument with his tongue in his cheek, but I am afraid that in this quarrel the theologian had the greater sense of humor of the two. Whatever we think about the nature of ultimate values, or whether such things actually exist, or whether they are valid of themselves or may be determined by some scientific method, this fact remains: most scientists are working with tools and methods that give only a partial glimpse of the real nature of any complex human and social problem. Each practical situation has in it some elements of the unique; each scientific method deals with uniform abstractions that tell less than the complete story.

Physical scientists often remark that the social sciences deal with problems that are full of value judgments and are therefore handicapped in adopting a truly scientific attitude. As a great physicist once said to me, "You social scientists make the mistake of trying to give the whole answer. If you, as a homeowner, want me to help you fix up a room, I can tell you as a scientist exactly how long and wide it is, and exactly how hot it is, and maybe what color the walls are. But the more I try to tell you how to arrange the furniture, the less I'll be acting like a scientist."

There is no question that difficulties arise when social scientists try to study for policy makers the problems of human behavior. Take, for example, the dilemma of the social scientist who tries to study the behavior of human beings under conditions of military service. A study of the critical problems in this field, if it is to be useful, must deal with many difficult and controversial issues. Should the races be segregated in the armed forces? What happens to the sexual behavior of millions of men under the artificial conditions of military life, and what should the military service do about it? Should convicted criminals be exempted from compulsory military services? If not, how should they be treated?

To questions like these science can produce no complete answers. It can give a relatively accurate picture of what happens now. It can tell a good deal about what would probably happen under various conditions in the future, especially in the smaller units of organization or with respect to particular aspects of each general question. But it cannot, with any scientific confidence, tell a Secretary of Defense or a military personnel officer precisely what he ought to do about any of these broad problems.

The social scientist who undertakes research for the operating official on problems of this nature is likely to run into plenty of difficulties that are not his fault and a few that characteristically are. The difficulties that are not his fault generally come from the tendency of the layman to think that he understands these problems as well as anyone else and his tendency not to see that exact research can contribute much to his business. But it will do the social sciences no harm to acknowledge that some of the difficulties arise because the social scientists have not always learned how to work in co-operation with operating officials.

This skill, it seems to me, consists largely in knowing the

limitations of one's own expertise. At some point in the process of studying and deciding on any social problem the boundaries of expert knowledge end, and the realm of responsible judgment begins. But all too often the scientist fails to recognize that he has gone beyond the boundaries of what can be proved by research and is speaking *ex cathedra* on matters on which his own judgment is just as personal, and perhaps nearly as prejudiced, as any layman's. Too often, too, he is likely to want both the confidential ear of the responsible official and the right to tell the academic world all about that relationship. It is impossible to maintain at the same time the privilege of the confidential adviser, which is that of making an unpopular recommendation in private, and the privilege of the neutral scientist, which is that of communicating freely with his colleagues and the general public.

Difficulties such as these arise in the social sciences when the scientist thinks that his specialty is the most important aspect of the total problem and ignores the broader considerations of policy that are involved. But the troubles of the social sciences in such respects are picayune by comparison with those of the natural sciences. The physical scientist or engineer is never backward about pushing his own specialty. The electronics engineer, for example, is as likely to think that all problems ought to be solved by electronic methods as a commanding general in any theater of operations is likely to think that his area holds the key to the whole war. The responsible administrator or operating official has to correct for these distortions with the help of advisers of broader competence. Indeed, the whole business of operations research is most useful as a means of testing the physical aspects of the problem in relation to the economic or administrative or procedural aspects—to discover whether the extra speed of a proposed new airplane is worth the price that is paid in weight or fuel, or whether the extra electronic equipment does not burden a plane and a pilot more than it will help.

Moreover, as soon as physical science gets out of the laboratory and classroom and begins to be applied to practical problems, its application is shot through with the most controversial types of policy and value judgments. The advisory machinery of the federal government has seen its most bitter battles waged round the heads of engineers and physicists—battles in which no one could tell just where scientific considerations ended and policy considerations began.

The General Advisory Committee of the Atomic Energy Commission, for example, deals with the most secret data and advises on the most secret problems in the United States government. It is made up of scientists and engineers of the very highest standing. When the decision was made by the Atomic Energy Commission and the President to proceed with the program of developing the H-bomb, its advice must have been sought. This decision was one that obviously involved a great many difficult scientific and economic questions, in addition to the broad moral and emotional problem whether it was desirable to create such an instrument of destruction. If there were ever any problem on which the highest public officials should accept their proper responsibility and on which scientific advisers should not be held accountable except for the accuracy of their scientific advice, this was the problem.

Yet in May 1953 this supersecret issue was the subject of an article in *Fortune* that charged that various members of the General Advisory Committee had opposed the decision to construct the H-bomb because of moral scruples, emotional prejudices, or a general desire to obstruct the mission of the Strategic Air Command. About the same time the Pentagon was full of gossip on the same problem—gossip in which the motives, the character, and the loyalty of individuals were brought into question. And related issues were breaking into the newspapers on several other fronts. On this range of problems I have no scientific competence whatever. But I am certain that published articles that attack the motives of scientific advisers will seriously weaken the government's ability to get scientific advice. And I believe with equal conviction that to publish such an attack, which leaves the scientific adviser quite unable to defend himself without talking in public about secret matters, is the height of unfairness.

Of all issues that the military planners must face with the aid of their scientific advisers, few can be as difficult as these twin issues: first, how to divide our resources (particularly, our fissionable material) between strategic bombing and tactical bombing or artillery, and, second, how to divide our resources between offensive and defensive purposes, especially in the air. The decisions on such issues must have a profound effect on the comparative roles and missions of the three military services. Indeed, the issues are broad enough to go beyond the competence of the military planner as well as that of the physical scientist; they involve diplomatic and economic considerations as well.

Such issues, during the past few years, have not been kept close secrets within the executive branch. Their broad outlines were sketched during 1952 and 1953 for anyone who took the trouble to read the newspapers and a few of the technical journals, even though the top political leaders did not lay them before the public.

For example, Hanson Baldwin discussed in the *New York Times* (June 5, 1952) the recommendations of Project Vista, a study undertaken by the California Institute of Technology. Vista, he reported, recommended the maximum possible use of atomic weapons for tactical purposes and took the side of the Army against the Air Force on several of their jurisdictional issues.

A little earlier the East River Project, in which some of the same scientists were involved, had made its reports, some of them publicly. This was a study undertaken by Associated Universities, Inc. (an institution that had been created largely to carry on research for the Atomic Energy Commission) under a contract with the Department of Defense, the Federal Civil Defense Administration, and the National Security Resources Board. The East River studies presented a frightening prospect —the possibility that some day an unexpected enemy air attack might saturate the defense and wipe out the major cities of the United States. This could be prevented, they argued, only if the military services could provide a more effective system of early warning and more effective interception and destruction of enemy planes than were presently being planned.

Again, some of the same scientists who worked on these studies took part during the summer of 1952 in a special Summer Study Group attached temporarily to the Lincoln Project. Lincoln is a continuing research and development program managed by M.I.T. for the Air Force. This Study Group made a number of recommendations, some of them proposing new research and development, others proposing the immediate installation of a new chain of radar stations across the Arctic to provide a distant early warning of any enemy air attack. The argument of some of the scientists was that a really effective air defense—including a distant early warning system—was essential to our national existence and had now become technically feasible. The view of the Air Force, on the other hand, was that the early warning program needed experimental and operational testing, and that until that testing had been done it was not safe or economical to proceed with the expenditure of so much money as a full immediate installation would require.[2]

Many of the technical aspects of this difference of opinion are military secrets. But the most interesting general administrative issue is not. That is the issue whether a group of scientists, having been commissioned and paid by a military service to study a problem vital to national security, is free to report on that problem to anyone other than its original clients.

What happened in this particular case? It may be assumed that the National Security Resources Board and the Federal Civil Defense Administration, both of which had every reason and right to be informed on such matters, followed up on the East River Study by keeping in touch with the work of the Lincoln Summer Study Group. It is certain that through some channels the Alsop brothers became well informed about the work of the Summer Study Group and its conclusions and wrote a series of newspaper and magazine articles on air defense that were in sympathy with that Group's recommendations and critical of the Air Force for neglecting air defense. Several prominent scientists, including some who had been connected with the East River and Lincoln studies, began to carry on a public or semipublic campaign of criticism of the Air Force for its failure to take advantage of new "technological break-throughs" and to provide the United States with an effective air defense. And the privately published *Air Force* magazine informs the public that this issue thus became one in

[2] For an account of this whole sequence of events, see "the Truth About Our Air Defense," in *Air Force*, May 1953; the two articles by Omar N. Bradley, "A Soldier's Farewell," *Saturday Evening Post*, August 22 and 29, 1953; an address by Dr. Lloyd V. Berkner before the National Conference of Editorial Writers, Boston, October 17, 1953; and Charles J. V. Murphy, "The U. S. as a Bombing Target," *Fortune*, November 1953. See also review of this last article entitled *"Fortune's* Own Operation Candor," *Bulletin of the Atomic Scientists*, IX, No. 10 (December 1953).

which the Air Force felt required to defend, in a public controversy, its point of view on what amounted to a secret war plan.

You need not be concerned here with the question whether anyone violated official security regulations by giving classified information to the Alsop brothers. If anyone were concerned, he could not find out, and if he could find out, he ought to understand that any possible offender was sinning in good company. Military research secrets appear in the newspapers not entirely as the result of journalistic ingenuity or of accidental disclosure. They are given to the newspapers, with or without the formality of declassification, by civilian officials and military officers who are seeking to advance the policies, to expand the missions, and to increase the appropriations of their respective services—sometimes at the expense of the other services.

We should rather be concerned with this question: Will the system of contractual research in private institutions prosper unless the contracting officers and the scientists have a common understanding of the scientist's proper role? Should the scientist ever be free to give his recommendations not only to the officer who contracted for them, but also to that officer's military superiors? Or, going outside the executive branch, to the Congress or to the general public?

The problem becomes particularly complicated in the case of the outside adviser, but it is difficult enough in any case. No simple answer has ever been given in the United States (by contrast, for example, with Great Britain) to govern the conduct in similar situations even of any administrative or scientific subordinate in the regular civil service. The first loyalty of the subordinate in the United States is not to his superiors in the executive hierarchy. It is not to the service as a body, except perhaps for a few members of the military and foreign services. It is certainly not to the Congress or to any political party. All these loyalties are secondary, even though they may be powerful and generally binding. The primary loyalty is to the Constitution of the United States, under which only the people are the ultimate power, and the individual official must sometimes judge for himself his relative obligations to the branches of the government and to the various levels of officialdom.

The written Constitution of the United States thus does not make for a rigid form of government by specifying the obligations of the government official in unmistakable form. On the contrary, it puts him in a position of frequently having to decide for himself on issues about which there would be no question in the mind of his British counterpart, who must operate under the much more rigid system of an unwritten constitution. Just as the formal allegiance of the British official is to the person of the King, his ultimate administrative loyalty is to the policies of the King in Council—in practical modern terms, the Cabinet—as interpreted for the civil service by the permanent corporate hierarchy of the Administrative Class. Hardly anything would justify the civil servant or the military officer for disobedience to those policies, or for suggesting to the Parliament or the public that he was not heartily in accord with them.

This relationship is so well understood that it generally works without sanctions, but it is so completely accepted that sanctions are available. A high-ranking British general whose experience had involved work in close acquaintance with the central policies of the government once told me that he had been so certain in 1938 that the Chamberlain policies were suicidal that he would have liked to resign his commission and tell the nation—using facts to back up his assertion—that it was in deadly danger. "But," he went on to say, "to prove my point I'd have had to use facts, and those facts were secret, and I could hardly have carried on my public campaign if I had been put in prison under the Official Secrets Act."

An American general or admiral has nowhere nearly so difficult a choice. He has many more possible courses of action. He can, if he is willing to run the risk of demotion or transfer, speak directly and boldly in opposition to current policy; he is especially likely to do so if he is near retirement anyhow. Or he can pass a hint to a Congressional committee that he is willing to talk if they summon him and twist his arm. Or he can simply see that his juniors pass the ammunition to his service's association of reserve officers, and let them act as guerrillas in the battles of public opinion. With the civil servant the freedom of action is even greater, since most civilians in relatively high positions are already accustomed to moving back and forth between government and private life. And, by comparison with his British counterpart, the civilian, like the military officer, is not effectively restrained by any laws of the United States regarding official secrets, just as the American newspaperman is not so effectively restrained by our easygoing laws of libel.

If this is true of the career officials of the United States, it is even more true of the scientist in a private institution who serves the government under contract. The nature of his intellectual pursuits makes him independent in his ideas; the nature of academic institutions makes him undisciplined in his working relationships; and the very device of the administrative contract, like his intellectual ancestors' idea of the social contract, is a means of escaping from a complete subordination to fixed authority.

But this lack of a fixed system and a rigid code makes it all the more necessary to develop a generally understood, though flexible, set of relationships. Admiral John Doe, let us say, is working on problems of antisubmarine warfare, and he contracts with Metropolitan University for a study by Dr. Richard Roe, a nuclear ichthyologist, on the possibilities of using fish to aid in the detection of submarines. Dr. Roe is sure that, by altering the breed of guppies somewhat, the problem will be solved and the nation will be saved. Admiral Doe looks at the technical data, thinks the odds are not too good, considers the method too expensive, believes it is not compatible with the new communications system of the antisubmarine fleet, and turns the idea down.

What should Dr. Roe do? Should he take the issue to the Secretary of the Navy or all the way to the President? Or should he content himself with muttering to colleagues who have been properly cleared, in meetings of naval advisory committees, about the stupidity of the high brass?

We ought always to assume that perhaps the high brass and their political superiors have been stupid, and that Dr. Roe may have the key to the nation's security, and that he may feel it necessary to go to the President on the matter—if the President will listen to him. After all, even Navy regulations provide that there are circumstances in which a junior officer is warranted in seizing command from a senior officer and putting him in the brig. But since the circumstances in which Dr. Roe is operating do not involve physical combat, and communications are relatively open, the least that he could do would be to keep Admiral Doe fully informed if he decided to operate out of channels and promote his ideas with the Admiral's superiors. This point of etiquette alone would clear up some of the problems of relationships.

But Dr. Roe, it seems to me, has another obligation. He ought to realize that his data can never be put into operation alone; they can become part of an operating program only when combined with administrative judgments regarding bud-

getary and legislative priorities, the capabilities of the administrative organization, the merits of competing technical possibilities, and a host of other factors. If he realizes this fact, he
will be more tolerant than most of his colleagues about the
shortcomings of the bureaucracy, both military and civilian.

Nevertheless the scientific adviser is sometimes in a quite
difficult dilemma. He is torn between his administrative obligation to stay within channels and his obligation as a citizen
to speak out on an important issue. Until a clearer code is
evolved and a more adequate corps of officials with responsibility for decisions has developed, it is hard to criticize the
scientists who think it their duty to take stands in public on
issues on which their knowledge qualifies them to speak.

There have been plenty of recent examples of vigorous and
effective criticism. For example, Dr. Lloyd V. Berkner, who
played a major part in both the East River and Lincoln Project
reports, summed up his ideas in a speech at the University of
Minnesota in September 1952, in which he argued strongly
that the basic strategy of the Air Force, that of emphasizing the
ability to retaliate with strategic bombing, needed to be sup-
plemented by the development of a really effective system of
air defense—a series of new technological break-throughs, he
reported, might make a sound air defense reasonably effective. In the same speech Dr. Berkner argued strongly that a
new organization like the O.S.R.D. ought to be created to give
the scientist the opportunity, without regard to military restrictions, to exploit to the fullest the new technological developments for military purposes.

Dr. Berkner's arguments were persuasive, but the very fact
that he made this speech and others like it partially disproved
one of his own points. "If the scientist presses his ideas at high
levels," he said, ". . . he is in the position of going over the
head of his boss, and of ending his usefulness to the Govern-

ment by incurring the enmity and displeasure of those who have supported him." The most significant thing about Dr. Berkner's speech was not what he said, but that he was willing to say it and able to say it without ending his usefulness to the government. For he was clearly, on the basis of his participation in two major studies financed by the military and defense agencies, challenging an important feature of current military policy.

The special studies made by universities and research institutions for military agencies could not have been made by institutions completely independent of government. They were too deeply involved in current military problems and required too much access to secret data to be made by scientists who were independent in the full sense of the word. But neither could they have been made by scientists in the regular chain of command. This is not to say that anyone in the chain of command is not free to tell the truth or to say what he thinks. It is undoubtedly true that men, even scientists, yield to such pressures, but that is not the point. The point is that the truth in such a matter is not the product of individual inspiration, or even of individual research. The truth—by which I mean the answer that most closely corresponds to the fullest accomplishment possible with existing resources—can be discovered only by elaborate research, and whether or not to pay for such research is a policy decision of the first order of magnitude.

Some other free nations have quite properly been critical about the way in which the United States has handled its political investigation of scientists during the years of the cold war. But such criticism ought to take this into account: the United States is the only nation that has ever been willing to support and create private institutions to make studies on problems combining scientific and military considerations—problems of a sort that would elsewhere be considered the very heart of general staff planning. The private institutions that are now largely supported by military funds are the most important sources of independent, skeptical, and uninhibited criticism of military thinking. And independent criticism is the basis of freedom in any political mechanism.

Some problems of a different nature arise as a government department seeks to make use of advice not from outside studies, but from advisers who become a part of its internal machinery.

As World War II came to an end Vannevar Bush, who had brought most of the nation's leading scientists into the war program through the O.S.R.D., sought to create machinery by which scientists could continue to make a contribution to military research during peacetime. The form that this effort took was first the Joint Research and Development Board, which Bush persuaded the Secretaries of War and Navy to create in 1946, and later its statutory successor, the Research and Development Board. The Board set up its subordinate machinery by creating committees in various specialized fields, such as electronics, ordnance, and aeronautics. Each of these committees included representatives from each of the military services, but it also included several eminent scientists from private life, one of them as chairman. These outside members were technically, of course, public officials. They were investigated, cleared, appointed, and sworn into office with as much formality as any full-time public official. But they typically worked at the job ten or fifteen days a year.

The job itself was to review the research programs of the military services, to advise the Department of Defense on ways in which those programs could be strengthened, and to bring into the military departments the most advanced thought of the scientist in private life.

Each of these fifteen or sixteen major committees set up subordinate panels and subpanels on much the same pattern and divided its general field among them. The Board, the committee, the panel, and the subpanel thus constituted a sort of hierarchy, the lower group attempting to settle issues by common agreement and passing on the more difficult decisions to the higher level for consideration.

This system had the advantage of forcing the military services to review their programs in the presence and under the criticism of relatively neutral outside experts. It continued the great accomplishment of O.S.R.D.: it kept many of the nation's most competent scientists in active association with the military services. That it did so even in peacetime was a tremendous accomplishment. But it must be acknowledged that some features of the system had certain marked disadvantages—disadvantages that led the Committee on Department of Defense Organization (in which Dr. Bush himself took a leading role) to propose in 1953 the abolition of the Board as such, a proposal in which the incumbent Chairman of R.D.B., Walter G. Whitman, concurred. Let me give my own personal view of those disadvantages.

First of all, it was necessary to set the committees up in such a way that the part-time consultant could make a contribution. A man who spends ten or fifteen days a year on a job can bring to it the expert knowledge he accumulates on his regular job, but he has very little time to add any extra expertise. This fact dictated the basic arrangement of the committees. It was possible to find experts in aeronautics and atomic energy in private life, and therefore possible to set up committees in such fields. But recruiting them meant that the basic machinery was geared to produce advice on subjects arising within those particular specialties. It may not have been well suited to produce the kind of advice most needed by the military services. The most important issues may well have been issues like these: What are the possibilities of developing totally new techniques of warfare, or totally new weapons, to solve the new operational problems of undersea warfare, or of air combat, or of amphibious landings? The real potential of science was to bring about really revolutionary changes in strategy or tactics within any one of these operational categories or types of combat. But a committee of specialists (in biological warfare, say, or in ordnance) was not likely to take such a broad view of the problem of the military strategist. It was certain to concentrate on its particular specialty, to think in terms of its established techniques, and to seek to expand them in competition with other specialties.

Consequently the Defense Department was always talking about changing the fundamental organization of the committees, to set them up by categories of warfare rather than by academic disciplines or scientific specialties. But the discussion always foundered on several stubborn facts. First, each category of warfare required so many specialized types of scientists as advisers that you could not get them all in the same room. Next, there were not enough scientists in each major specialty (for example, electronics) to spread them over all the categories of warfare. Finally, the average part-time scientist had very little to contribute to the tactical problems of the several operational categories. The inevitable conclusion was that the full-time staff of the Board had to take the responsibility for gearing the advice of the scientists into the plans of the operating officers. This required an intimate relation with the services and with the Joint Chiefs of Staff that it was never possible to develop.

As a result the Research and Development Board, although it was the highest echelon in the scientific structure of the

Department of Defense, did very little to lead the Department to take a unified look at the future of whole systems of weapons in relation to strategy. Instead, it tended to bog down in a detailed review of the specific scientific programs of the military departments and in efforts to prevent overlapping and duplication among them. In short, the very nature of the system forced the consideration, at the highest level in the hierarchy, of specialties that should have been handled by subordinates.

This drawback was made worse by a certain amount of fencing between the scientists and the military. This was partly a result of the general feeling of each of two types of experts that its respective skills were the more important. But it also took the particular form of a competition over precise issues of organization and procedure.

In this respect the O.S.R.D. precedents may have been misleading. The O.S.R.D. had been a tremendous success because it competed aggressively with the military research agencies. It brought in private scientists, gave them full authority, went directly to high political officers (from the President down) on disagreements with military officers, and used its own judgment in deciding which weapons to try to develop. Something of the same approach carried over into the Research and Development Board, and did not work. The O.S.R.D. had brought in leading scientists on the theory that you must not ask important people to do a job unless you give them an appropriate amount of authority. The R.D.B. tried to apply the same principle with unhappy results. The committees were first set up with charters that promised them control over their own organization and their own staff and gave them authority to make binding decisions on matters within their field of interest. The outside scientists who served as chairmen and as members of all these committees and panels therefore came to expect that they, working with their fellow members from the military services, could make basic decisions in the military research program.

It did not work that way. First of all, the committees themselves could not keep their organization and staffs independent. It was impossible to define their respective subject matter in any way that kept them from overlapping hopelessly. Some superior authority—the Board or its Chairman—had to decide on the respective jurisdiction of the various committees, to decide on their budgets, and to appoint and supervise their personnel. More important, the Secretary of Defense, when facing an issue that had to be decided immediately, would ask the Chairman of the Research and Development Board for advice that had to be given without waiting for the clumsy machinery of subpanels, panels, and committees to come into action. There was therefore always the tendency for the Chairman of the Board, as a staff assistant to the Secretary of Defense, to make use of the committee staffs as expert consultants in their respective fields—a practice that usually made the committees feel that they were being bypassed and made their military members protest that decisions had been made affecting their interests without giving them a chance to be heard.

Even more important, the committees were in an impossible position when they believed that they could take action cutting across the main chain of command. Yet this anomaly was clearly involved in their belief that they could make decisions about the military research and development program. It would be possible—although fantastically ineffective—to centralize the military research and development programs under a series of committees and take them entirely away from the military services. But as long as the research programs are paid for out of money appropriated to the military departments and administered by men in the military chain of command, a committee headed by part-time outsiders simply could not make the basic decisions on those programs. Indeed, they were likely to find that the effort to review those programs comprehensively occupied their time so completely that they could not give very useful advice as part-time specialists.

The effort, moreover, to make this type of committee control authoritative set up counterpressures. The military departments, in order to resist control from the outside, effectively smothered the advisory machinery of the Research and Development Board.

They did so by developing a very clear theory of procedures and tactics. The basis was the theory that the military planners had to decide what scientific research work was needed—in technical terms, had the authority to determine "requirements." They then extended this theory, to which no one could possibly object in general terms, to argue that the R.D.B. committees did not even have the right to suggest changes in the detailed statements of requirements that would make it easier for scientists and engineers to get substantially the same results with greater certainty or more economy.

At the same time they properly insisted that the committees and panels could not make decisions except by unanimous agreement, and that disagreements would have to be referred up to the next echelon and on to the Board itself. This requirement was administratively proper, but hardly necessary to protect the interests of each of the services. The military members of the committees—not because they were military men, but because they were full-time professionals—were generally not at all inclined to submit their own programs to the control of a group led by part-time consultants from outside the government. Even under a system of majority voting, if such a thing had been possible, the military members of a committee would almost certainly have closed ranks against any authoritative control of their respective programs by the committee. But this outcome was made all the more certain when a single vote of objection would send the issue up the line to the Board for final decision.

This outcome was seen the most clearly in the effort to use the Board and its committees to prevent overlapping and duplication among research programs. The effort to allocate particular research programs to particular military departments was for a time the principal method used to push for economy in military research. This effort, however, bogged down completely. The basic reason was that each military service was competing for jurisdiction—in military terms, for "roles and missions"—with the other services. As it did so, it saw in scientific research the essential key to the development of its tactics and strategy in such a way as to increase its own importance in competition with the other services. For this reason no service was willing to entrust to any other the conduct of its research program.

But in addition to this basic reason the effort to allocate programs bogged down because of the way in which it was organized. It bogged down because each committee was thought of as something like a court, and each issue was expected to be decided by the presentation of a case, the hearing of opposing witnesses, and the vote of the committee or the Board.

Dr. Conant has argued that the military research program needs to be reviewed by some semijudicial procedure that would pass on scientific proposals, hear both sides of the case, and then make a binding decision.[3] With his argument that both sides of a proposal should be carefully presented and considered I am in full agreement. But the nub of the problem

---

[3] James B. Conant, *Modern Science and Modern Man* (New York: Columbia University Press, 1952), p. 68.

is how to set up the authority to make the decision, after both sides have been presented. In the R.D.B. the effort to allocate functions could not work by a judicial type of formal procedure, because the R.D.B. lacked all the elements of independent authority that must be the backbone of any judicial system. The jury—in this case the R.D.B. committee—was not made up of persons who were selected to avoid any connection with the case. It was made up of the litigants themselves. There was no independent judge. And the government had to rely on the evidence presented by the rival parties instead of having its own attorney to present the case for the public interest.

But the essential difficulty was that the control of the research programs was being managed in an aggressive way by the military services, which prepared the plans, let the contracts, and received the appropriations. By comparison with their dynamic management a slow and clumsy system of review by three or four layers of committees could hardly have caught up with the parade, even if all committee members had been eager to do so.

The Chairman of the Research and Development Board, Mr. Whitman, undertook in 1952 a considerable reorganization of these relationships. A new charter from the Secretary of Defense gave him a more definite responsibility for advising the Secretary (especially on the financial aspects of the research program) independently of the Board, and using the committee staff members as his personal staff. He issued a new set of rules of organization and procedure defining the functions of the committees, making it clear that their role was advisory rather than authoritative, but on the other hand affirming their duty to question the details of military requirements. The new system seemed to get general approval from both the military and the scientists. But before it had been thoroughly tested the

Research and Development Board itself had been abolished and its place taken by two new Assistant Secretaries of Defense.[4]

We have already discussed the issues raised when political attacks are made on the integrity of science. Some equally difficult problems arise when scientists, by serving as advisers, put themselves in the position of working at the same time for a private employer and for the government, in situations in which conflicts of interest may arise.

These problems are particularly difficult when they are not faced squarely. It is very difficult for scientists to face them squarely when they are quite aware that they are serving the government part-time at a personal sacrifice or when their organizations are making them available without reimbursement. It is also easy for situations to arise in which the only way whereby adequate skills can be made available is through a procedure in which a conflict of interest is inherent. For example, as World War II came to an end the first important issue of government organization regarding science that arose was this: how should the government arrange to declassify the secret materials in possession of the O.S.R.D.? The leaders in the O.S.R.D. urged that the government commission the National Academy of Sciences to recommend which items should be made public and which should be continued under military secrecy. The Academy had been chartered by the Congress for just such purposes; it was impossible to hold the O.S.R.D. together for such a dull peacetime job; and the same scientists who had worked in the O.S.R.D. during the war, generally at great personal sacrifice, could work under Academy auspices to guide the declassification of their materials.

This idea was nevertheless opposed by Harold D. Smith,

4 The new Assistant Secretary of Defense for Research, Mr. Donald A. Quarles, outlined his plan for the reorganization of the Research and Development Committee structure in an address before the Institute of Industrial Research, in Detroit, on October 26, 1953.

then Director of the Budget. He believed that many of the wartime secrets might have tremendous influence on the development of industry, and hence on the fortunes of particular corporations. Looking at the list of officers and leading members of the National Academy and Research Council, he argued that if that agency were given a determining voice in the declassification of wartime secrets, some of its leading figures would be open to the charge that they had made public those discoveries that would benefit their corporations and suppressed those that would harm their corporations instead of being guided by an undivided concern for the national interest.

Accordingly the President assigned the responsibility for declassification to the Office of War Mobilization and Reconversion, which in turn put the actual conduct of the work in the Department of Commerce.[5]

The types of problems with which government advisory committees deal and the new system of administration by contract make it very hard to apply the old rules for the prevention of conflicts of interest. During the war the O.S.R.D. could not have done its job at all if a great many scientists had not been willing to run the risk of prosecution for violating minor aspects of the conflict-of-interest statutes.

After the war some of these were relaxed somewhat, but the Department of Justice began to be concerned about the way advisory committees were created and operated. The most difficult problems arose, not in the research field, but in the large-scale procurement of munitions and in mobilization planning. The Department of Justice feared that industrial groups would use such committees, even if set up with the best of intentions, to further monopoly. In 1950 the Deputy Attorney General, Peyton Ford, sent letters to all departments and

---

[5] Irvin Stewart, *Organizing Scientific Research for War* (Boston: Little, Brown and Co., 1948), pp. 288-89.

agencies concerned to outline the terms under which advisory committees should function.

Among these were the requirements that the government should draw up the agenda for committee meetings, should furnish a chairman for such meetings, and should keep the committees purely advisory in status, in order to retain in the hands of government officials the responsibility for action.[6]

Each of the principal research agencies has an advisory panel or a committee to help it develop its research policies, and perhaps subcommittees and subordinate panels of consultants to give it advice on the letting of contracts with particular institutions. In creating such advisory committees the government agencies have had to walk a tightrope in order to follow the rules of the Department of Justice on the one hand and, on the other hand, to consult the most eminent experts in the field. Their main safeguard, as far as the Department of Justice is concerned, is that the making of a contract with a research institution is the responsibility of the contracting officer, who in the Department of Defense is a full-time official. But even so it is not a simple matter to apply the standards of the Department of Justice in ways that make sense in practical situations.

These standards are based on the assumption that the representative of a private institution on an Advisory Committee is automatically involved in conflicts of interest, while the full-time official is not. This assumption is valid enough for the typical industry advisory committee, but it hardly fits most of the scientific advisory committees that we have been discussing. There are vested interests within the executive branch as well as among private firms.

An agency in the office of the Secretary of Defense, for

6 *Study of Monopoly Power, Hearings before the Subcommittee on Study of Monopoly Power of the Committee on the Judiciary. House of Representatives, Eighty-Second Congress, First Session, Serial No. 1, and Part 4, The Mobilization Program,* p. 172.

example, may find that its most difficult relationships are not with private contractors, but with the Army, the Navy, and the Air Force. The services are forced to compete in the political arena for their respective "roles and missions," because the Congress has not been willing to delegate authority to determine roles and missions to the responsible civilian executives—or to permit a civilian executive to develop the stability and the staff necessary to do the job. In such a case the Secretary of Defense or his agent may properly turn to a scientist from a quite disinterested agency—and in this context an important industry as well as a university may be disinterested—to get impartial advice in the public interest.

It was perhaps for this reason that in 1952 the Secretary of Defense created a study group on continental defense, under the chairmanship of Dr. M. J. Kelly of the Bell Telephone Laboratories, to advise him on the problems of air defense in which bitter disputes had arisen among the services and between them and a number of the private scientists.

Similarly, the distinction between the private citizen and part-time consultant on the one hand and the full-time government officer on the other is a poor guide in determining conflicts of interest. The part-time consultant may represent an industrial corporation interested only in increasing its profits, or he may represent one that is taking on a government research contract only out of a sense of duty or scientific interest. On the other hand, the full-time official may be either completely dedicated to the public service or looking for the opportunity to create a career for himself in a university or private business.

If the distinction between public and private is no longer a clear-cut criterion, neither is the distinction between profit-making and nonprofit. Many a university (public or private) is so deeply dependent on defense contracts for the support of its scientific programs that it could not possibly take a detached view with regard, say, to the question whether basic research deserves federal support. As for industrial corporations, government contracting officers are properly alert to keep their profits to a reasonable figure, but profits may be in many cases the least important way in which a corporation may abuse the public interest. Many a scientific field involves research that could be used either for military purposes or for the development of skills that could be turned to commercial purposes. A corporation might undertake a research program without taking any profit whatever, entirely for the motive of building up its accumulation of skills and its scientific personnel in order to improve its competitive position in the industry; indeed, it might push a line of research, ostensibly for military purposes, that was really designed to solve commercial problems. If this abuse does not take place very often, it is because of the general integrity and public spirit of the executive and scientific personnel in both industry and the military departments, for abuses of this kind could never be detected by the typical auditor or investigator.

The most difficult conflict of interest with respect to advisory machinery comes potentially from inside the government— from political pressure brought to bear through the Congress. In the Department of Agriculture the Congress has generally prevented political competition for research money either by the old technique of cutting the melon in equal shares or by apportioning the money among the states according to some formula; for example, in proportion to the rural population of the states. The other federal research agencies are eager to avoid political interference with research contracts, but they also hope to avoid any such rigid apportionment of funds, which restricts their freedom in getting the research done in the most efficient manner. For this reason they have been eager to build up their political defenses by making arrangements that are obviously impartial. At the same time the sheer magnitude of the work and the lack of an adequate supply of scientific talent in the civil service have led the research agencies to call on the help of the leading scientific institutions in setting up their advisory machinery.

For example, the Office of Naval Research, when it established its Biological Sciences Advisory Board, made a contract with the National Academy of Sciences in establishing and maintaining such a board. In selecting names for this board the Navy insisted not only on representation from the major scientific fields involved, but also on the Board's including adequate geographical distribution and representation from various kinds of institutions (such as medical colleges and arts and science colleges).

Similarly, the Air Force, in appointing the Industry and Educational Advisory Board, called for nominations of six members by the Aircraft Industries Association and of two members (to represent educational institutions) by the Chairman of the Scientific Advisory Board of the Air Force. More recently the Air Research and Development Command made a contract with the National Academy of Sciences to advise it concerning the kind of advisory structure needed by the Air Force for its basic research program.

The most important problems of conflict of interest in the relationship of government and science are much more subtle than in the relationships with business and industry. They turn much more often on varying professional backgrounds, on differences among specialized careers, and on different conceptions of public interest than on any issue of profiteering.

The responsible executive has to be on his guard equally against the military officer who is sure that his own branch of the service could virtually win the next war alone and against the scientific specialist who thinks only of his particular academic discipline. The responsible executive is vulnerable to such special pressures because of the weakness in American government of general administration. This weakness leads both the scientific specialist and the military career corps to work for forms of organization that would require the executive to act only after receiving their advice—or, if possible, only in accord with their advice.

In British constitutional history the right to advise was gradually transformed into the right to make binding decisions. This transition was accomplished by the pressure of political parties and by the control of the public purse. In a much more scattered way something of the same kind takes place within the diffuse machinery for advice on scientific problems in the United States government. The force that pushes in this direction is not political in a partisan sense and does not depend on the ultimate control of the purse. It comes instead from the professional specialist's distrust of the general administrator or the politician. The electronics engineer or the chemist distrusts the military officer in an administrative position over him, and the general staff officer distrusts the judgment of the politician at the head of his department. Since many important issues can be decided only on the basis of organized study, and since for many reasons it is impossible to have competing studies, the right to conduct the study or prepare the plan becomes almost equivalent to the final authority to decide. The executive's only opportunity for control is then the very general and long-range one of controlling the nature of the advisory or planning machinery and the selection of its top personnel.

These tendencies on the part of the specialist are encouraged by the tendency of Congressional committees to support the specialist against the general executive. Thus a Congressional committee may criticize the President for not following the warnings of the Joint Chiefs of Staff, and by political pressure may attempt to make the judgment of subordinate advisers binding on their responsible superiors.

This takes us out of the question of how to organize to get scientific advice from private sources for the government official and leads us into the much more difficult question how the government may be organized, in its regular administrative system, to make the best use of the potentialities of science in furthering public policies.

VI

THE
STRUCTURE OF POLICY

A couple of centuries ago a government of laws and not of men was the ideal of those who distrusted arbitrary power. They hoped to make human affairs conform more closely to natural law, which was the will of God as manifest in nature. By the time of the Declaration of Independence Thomas Jefferson seemed to be drawing a distinction between the laws of nature and those of nature's God; it may have been only a rhetorical repetition, but he appealed to both to justify rebellion. Whatever he may have meant by the distinction, his scientific successors have put much less emphasis on the laws of God and have hoped to find ways to make use of the laws of nature to reduce the influence of caprice or guesswork in the government of society.

Since 1776 scientists have come down from the lofty philosophical interests of a Thomas Jefferson to deal with a great many specific problems of government. The efforts to apply science to social problems, for example, have been at the heart of our national programs for the improvement of agriculture and the development of our resources. They have stimulated the development of city planning and the hope that business management and public administration may create something like a science of organization. And most recently the techniques of operations research, by bringing the mathematical and physical sciences into closer co-operation with economic and sociological studies, have gone far beyond those of management engineering in their depth and precision.

It is no wonder that many a social scientist, looking at the spectacular accomplishments of the natural scientist, begins to dream of a society in which scientific method will replace the accidents of politics or the arbitrary decisions of administrators in determining the policies of society. Even an occasional natural scientist shares this idea; Julian Huxley, for example, looks forward to the time when "the essentially amateur politician and administrator of today will have been replaced by a new type of professional man, with specialized training. Life will go on against a background of social science."[1]

Are there, indeed, any limitations on the use of science to guide the decisions of government? Why should not every major policy decision be based on scientific findings? Why should not every major executive be guided by an authoritative scientific adviser? Ultimately, why should not a scientist be chosen, by scientific techniques, to occupy every position of power?

This is putting the question in its extreme form. I do so not to try to reduce it to an absurdity, but to take a look at its general outlines before discussing some specific and very practical issues that have arisen during the past few years with respect to science and public policy.

In dealing with this question it may be helpful not to speak in ideal or absolute terms. I do not think that it is enough to say that a system that would have major policy issues determined by science would be undemocratic and would deny any freedom of choice to the majority of the people—even if that

[1] Julian Huxley, *Man in the Modern World* (New York: New American Library, 1952), pp. 120-21.

happens to be true. The scientist likes to think in quantitative and pragmatic terms. Is there any way to approach this question in such terms? Let me try.

I have to start with a couple of assumptions. The first is the idea that there is a government, and that it has an executive head. The second is that the executive must give some measure of direction to the whole organization through some kind of organized structure, in which he deals mainly with the heads of major departments, and each of them in turn deals with his subordinates through a hierarchical and subdivided structure. An organization chart is a very crude (usually a deceptively crude) model of such a hierarchy. Each of the millions of persons at the bottom level of this pyramid is different from every other; his work and his abilities are unique. The process of administration is to identify or imagine some uniform patterns; to set up general standards and general goals; and to select for consideration at the top the individual issues of the most general significance, so that decision on them will give the greatest amount of effective direction to the organization as a whole. This process is largely one of synthesis—of creating a singleness of organization and program out of a natural diversity. If you start at the bottom of the organization chart, you must go on combining slightly dissimilar things until you have established a quite artificial and arbitrary unity.

If the organization chart is the model of a government, a university curriculum is the crude model of science. Here the process works in the direction, not of artificial integration, but of natural division and subdivision. The scientist is an analyst. He breaks each scientific discipline down into subdisciplines and multiplies their subordinate specialties. He does not deal with the total aspect of any practical problem; he has to analyze it into a great many abstract parts, and what he learns about any part of the problem opens up a tremendous number of further questions that call for solution. If you start a scientist on a simple concrete problem, he can build on top of it an inverted pyramid of abstract specialized sciences and refined research projects.

When you try to match up the pyramid of the government organization with the inverted pyramid of science, you are bound to run into trouble.

It is true, no doubt, that in the higher reaches of abstract science new unities are discovered—simpler patterns that account for the great diversity of the things that appear on the surface. In much the same way, it is true in religion that the Christian ethic can be summed up in two commandments that take the place of the Decalogue and Deuteronomy, which in turn were simpler than the even more rigid and detailed customary laws of earlier and more primitive cultures. But unhappily it is not possible to relate these grand abstractions to the immediate problems of public affairs in any very practical system of organization. The most important truths can be dealt with only by the individual mind and the individual conscience. We are still faced, then, with this problem: At the lowest levels of the government hierarchy the worker must deal with problems each of which could be solved perfectly, as an individual problem, only by a considerable number of scientists; and in the process of solution each of those scientists would open up enough new questions, all needing to be answered before a final solution could be obtained, to keep their research going indefinitely.

I have already spoiled my effort to put this discussion in quantitative terms by letting my answer reach infinity. In practice, of course, nothing of this sort happens, because very few scientists are interested in pure science. Most of them are partly engineers at heart; they want to use the scientific method, or rather some particular scientific method, to solve the key part or a new part of some problem, while they rely on arbitrary policy, general experience, tradition, or guesswork to fill in the gaps.

As they do so they are likely to notice that the higher in government an issue goes for decision, the less likely it is that it can be answered by scientific research. Some will argue that this is not so. A very eminent diplomat, in a moment of exasperation, once remarked to me that if the hierarchical pyramid of the State Department were turned upside down, the only result anyone would notice would be that the typing would not be done very well. In a similar mood a scientist might argue that the reason why scientific issues are not taken to the top of an organization is that the executives are not competent to handle them.

This is doubtless a true reason, but it is not the only reason, or the effective one. A better reason is that only in the lower reaches of the government pyramid do problems become specialized enough to correspond to the structure of specialization of the sciences and to the specialized training of the scientist.

In the lower levels of the pyramid of policy the problem may be mainly scientific—that is to say, it may be a problem that can be solved by the precise research methods of one of the sciences. How can an explosive be made more powerful? What kind of testing process will identify the man with the fastest reaction time? What can be done to make an airplane fly faster? These are questions that science can take hold of. To get an airplane that will fly faster you put to work an aeronautical engineer, or rather a propulsion engineer and an aerodynamic engineer, supported by a number of more specialized colleagues. Their purposes and their skills correspond to the purposes of certain very specialized subdivisions of several government agencies.

Just a little higher on the pyramid of government policy

the sciences begin to give less precise answers, and usually in terms of statistical probability rather than absolutes, because the questions themselves are of a different nature: What combination of bomb load and fuel load should a bomber of a certain type have in order to get the maximum speed, with acceptable armor protection, at which pilots may be expected to fly with reasonable safety? At this level a number of different types of scientists need to work together on operations research, which in turn must be guided by a number of policy assumptions supplied by operating officials.

Finally, when you go still farther toward the top of the organization, the problems begin to frustrate science completely: What proportion of our resources shall be put into bombing planes, by comparison with land forces or naval vessels or air defense? How much shall we rely on building up supplies of weapons, and how much on encouraging a stable economy? How do we appraise the intentions of any potential enemy?

Much more often than not, the controlling elements in the vast web of government decisions (even though they may well be questions on which it is important to have the advice of scientists, or on which men with scientific background ought to make the decisions with full executive authority) are least likely to be the questions that can readily be answered precisely by scientific research. Aerodynamics has been one of the more dynamic of the sciences in its social consequences. Yet the way in which it will make its contribution is often prescribed by the answer to the questions being considered at the next higher level of the pyramid. Whether applied research in that field will receive support and what problems it will be asked to consider will depend (in the hypothetical example we have been using) on decisions about the bombing system as a whole and about the relative demands of speed and range and armament and maneuverability. And as we look at still higher levels on the pyramid of government it is clear that whether we develop more long-range bombers or more battleships or interceptor planes will depend mainly on the military strategists, and that whether we develop any of them (and how many) will depend on the still less scientific judgments of the diplomats and the politicians about our views of other nations and on our decision concerning how much national armament is required for national security.

Scientific methods are the most useful in determining *how* a specific thing is to be done; the more specific the thing, the more precise the determination. They are less often and less immediately useful in determining *whether* or *when* such things are to be done and *how much* effort or money is to be spent on them. But these are the controlling decisions, the decisions that must be made in the upper levels of the hierarchy if a government is to have any unity of purpose and action. This necessity, too, leads the higher officials to deal with the less scientific aspects of their major problems.

A final reason is one that has to do with the way in which responsibilities are delegated in any organization. Any issue that can be reduced to precise and objective terms is one that a superior can delegate with confidence to a subordinate. No matter how intricate and difficult the operation, no matter how much skill and training may be required for its performance, the executive will be willing to delegate it to a subordinate if there are precise standards to use in judging its performance. Just as you permit a clerk to handle money because you can audit his accounts, you permit a junior bacteriologist to inspect the water supply on which the health of a city depends because you can tell him (on the basis of definite professional standards) exactly how many and what varieties of bacteria can be tolerated.

But then we come to questions that, step by step, become less objective in their nature. How many bacteria can the water system tolerate? How much should the city spend on reducing infant mortality by public health measures? How much salary should it pay the public health officer? These questions become progressively more difficult to answer in precise numerical or objective terms; more difficult to answer in ways that others can readily check by methods on which there is a professional consensus; more dependent on factors on which research does not give a conclusive and verifiable answer and on which the scientist's opinion may be as prejudiced as any layman's.

For the sake of simplicity I have been talking as if each problem in government were either precise and scientific or the opposite. This alternative, of course, is not so. Most problems of any importance are made up of a mixture of factors, some of which can be stated in quite precise terms and tested by objective research, while others are much more vague and general and more dependent on interests, values, and ideals. Any system of staff work for an executive then becomes a sort of sieve, screening out those aspects of the problems that can more nearly be solved by science (as well as the quite different category of problems that are not important enough) and bringing to the executive for decision only those aspects of the problem that he is not willing to delegate.

This relationship means, of course, that a much lower level of purely intellectual ability may be required for the decisions that come to the top of the government pyramid than for those that are made nearer the bottom. I suppose that it took much more detailed knowledge of the latest specialized discoveries in nuclear physics, and greater concentration on the purely scientific aspects of the program, to do the work of many a junior scientist at Los Alamos than to do the work of Dr. Bush or General Groves, who had top-level responsibilities for atomic development. And they, in turn, needed to know a great deal more about the scientific aspects of the atomic bomb than did the President of the United States. When the President made at Potsdam the fateful decision to use the bomb he may have been right or wrong, but whether he was right or wrong was surely not the result of a lack of scientific advice or understanding. For the scientists themselves divided immediately and bitterly on just that type of issue, and are still divided, apparently according to the same kind of idealistic or temperamental differences that characterize the rest of us.

But, you may say, this confusion occurs because our social sciences are relatively backward; as soon as we develop a real science of society and human behavior the highest issues of policy can then be settled by scientific techniques.

There are many social scientists who believe that the distinction between science and values is not a real one. They think that any true values can be determined by the processes of research; that only the relative backwardness of the social sciences has kept these sciences from determining them sooner; and that it is mere superstition to suppose that there are any values that are valid otherwise.

I am something of a skeptic about this point of view, but I should like to assume it to be true to see what effect it would have on the things we have been considering. If it is true, does it mean that in the long run, when the social sciences have reached an advanced state of development—or even a theoretically perfect state of development—decisions at the highest level of government may be determined by the scientific approach?

I do not believe that such determination is possible; indeed, I think it is quite likely that the greater the advances of sciences of all kinds, including the social sciences, the more difficult will be the burdens of responsibility and of judgment that will be placed on the principal executives in government. The advance over the centuries in science and technology has multiplied the number and the difficulty of choices that lie before the political leader. The King under Sir James Frazer's Golden Bough may have been marked for sacrifice in the end, but in the meantime he had few tough decisions to make; everything was settled by custom, status, and tradition. Maine remarked that the change from primitive to modern society was summed up in the change from status to contract. Since then we have moved on to a society in which the fate of people is determined even more by politics. In such a society, commanding the potential forces of modern technology, the modern executive and the legislator must make decisions every day that would have justified a major crisis in the politics of the nineteenth century.

In short, scientific discoveries do not restrict the scope of political and administrative discretion any more than they reduce the possibilities of further scientific research. On the contrary, they enlarge the opportunities and broaden the possibilities for discretionary judgment in governmental affairs, just as they do for the acquisition of further knowledge.

Leading scientists and industrialists are properly fond of noting that science has provided an endless frontier of technical development, since economic opportunities expand with every new discovery. At the same time every new change in our national system of economy or technology brings a few more policy issues to the harried government official.

As new technology creates new social problems the governmental executive may solve a few by asking scientists to provide him with the answers. But there will always be at least three reasons why he cannot submit all questions to research to get the answers.

The first is that some types of question call for an immediate answer—the kinds of question on which inaction or delay is itself an answer, and the worst kind. As long as there is conflict in human affairs this type of question will remain important. President Truman at Potsdam could not have referred to a study commission the issue whether to drop the bomb. On the other hand, many an executive has discovered an easy way to avoid doing something that he has decided not to do. The way is simply to appoint a research committee to study the matter until the issue has cooled off, and then to advise him why he should not do it.

The second reason is that each question, if it is to be answered by formal research, leads to another. It is a matter of infinite regression. You cannot get anywhere if you first make a complete study of what you ought to study; and then a complete study of the methods that you ought to use in making the study; and then a complete study of the way in which the results of your study should be applied. By that time, of course, you would need to study the extent to which changes in the situation had made the original question obsolete. Studies of all these types are, within limits, useful and necessary, but only by the application of arbitrary judgment can the process be shortened to such a point that it can be applied to the problems of the real world.

Third, there is the question how to take into account the political implications of a research project. It is a sign of political maturity—from the point of view of one who has faith in both democracy and the freedom of science—when the public is willing to accept and support the findings of science in its proper fields. But it is important to remember that some societies have not been willing to do so at all and that no society has been willing to do so all the time. Even in our own country today there are a great many forces that are willing to attack science in order to prevent it from even considering certain subjects.

As long as people like power, and some have more than others, the very decision to undertake a study on a given subject may be a major political decision. Certainly the terms of reference of the study and the selection of the personnel to make the study are political decisions. That is to say, they are decisions that must be based on discretionary if not arbitrary judgment. This is not to say that the appointment of personnel for a study is always made with intent to determine the answers; even in a public study of a highly political subject, it may be greatly in the interest of the appointing authority to select men whose objectivity and balanced judgment will give wisdom and weight to their recommendations. But major official commissions of inquiry on public affairs are not likely to be selected in the near future on the basis of competitive objective examinations.

If you think this proves only a deficiency on the part of mere politicians that will be remedied by the advance of science, I suggest that you discuss with the authorities of any university just how they make up their curriculum and just how they distribute their budgets among their various departments. I have heard hints that these processes are not conspicuously more scientific, objective, and passionless than comparable processes in the national government.

A few decades ago political reformers were greatly impressed with the possibilities of the initiative and the referendum. With an informed electorate, the more democracy the better, and nothing would be so democratic—so they reasoned—as letting the people themselves decide on various issues. But the lesson of experience with the initiative and the referendum is that too much depends on who frames the questions, and who decides when to submit them, and who decides how to reconcile them with other questions, to make this a very satisfactory method of determining policies. In short, we have had to learn all over again the fundamental principles of representative government. These principles are related, I believe, to the point that we were discussing a moment ago—that scientific issues tend to be delegated to lower levels of the government pyramid, while the higher authorities have to make the few controlling decisions in much more general terms.

And, for the reasons that we have just been discussing, no decision is so controlling as the selection of top personnel. This is the most important way in which a chief executive can control his departments. It is also the most important way in which the electorate can control the chief executive and the legislature. At the apex of the pyramid the issues are reduced, in effect, to a choice between candidates, and the democracies in which popular control has been the most real and the most effective have been those in which the people are limited, in their formal power, to a choice between two major parties. It has always seemed to me that some of the most able atomic scientists have overstated their case in arguing that the public ought to demand to know more about the details of our atomic energy program—how the bomb is made, how many bombs we have, and what we plan to do with them. I am inclined to think that, on the contrary, we should consider that most of these matters—like all the most delicate diplomatic negotiations and all the most important war plans—have to be left to the proper legislative and executive authorities, and that we should concentrate our attention on getting better ones. I personally do not want to know how many atomic bombs we have, and the figure would not mean much to me if I knew it. I do want to know that the bomb and the processes of planning for its custody and its possible use are fully under the control of properly constituted authorities who are effectively responsible to the people. Responsibility to the people, I must add, means that the key decisions of the executive authorities should be subject to the criticism of an adequate number of well-informed and independent experts and to the criticism and control of the legislators who may draw their technical advice from those experts.

But even if we are not on our way toward a system in which science takes the place of political responsibility and executive leadership, we are clearly well along in an era in which political leaders and administrators can further public policies far more effectively by making adequate use of science. And we have certainly developed a system of government in which more and more of our administrators, and perhaps some of our political leaders, will begin their careers as scientists or at least will have some training in science.

As we move in these directions a number of issues arise. Who should decide what research a government scientist will do? How should his recommendations be brought to the attention of high policy officials? Should some scientists be set apart from the regular system of departmental organization to enable them to push their research farther and faster than would be permitted them by the regular administrative system? Let us look briefly at two or three of the practical ways in which such problems have arisen in recent years, particularly in the Department of Defense.

In the military departments one of the most frequent debates between officers and scientists turns on the issue of "requirements." Scientific work on the development of a particular weapon is normally authorized by the statement of a military requirement for such work—a procedure that keeps the initiative, so to speak, under the control of officers with operating responsibility and training, rather than of the scientists themselves.

Now it is perfectly reasonable to say that, as a general rule, the scientist who is working for the military department ought to work on what the military department thinks it needs—that is to say, that military research should follow a statement of of military requirements. This is the procedural guarantee that research will concentrate on actual military needs. But it is a very different thing to make this general rule into an invariable rule. And it is still another thing to say that the scientist must not only work in accord with the official requirements, but ought not even to offer advice on them.

As far as advice is concerned, the position of the scientist—whether he is civilian or in uniform—is vastly stronger than it was before World War II. In each of the military services a research and development organization with no responsibility for current operations has direct access to high authority. The Office of Naval Research and the Assistant Chief of Naval Operations for Readiness; the Deputy Chief of Staff of the Air Force for Development; and the Chief of Research in the Office of the Chief of Staff of the Army; all now have functions as independent advisers of the military top command that were formerly buried in lower echelons.

This change in the structure of military organization merely reflects the change in the importance that the generals and admirals attach to science and technology. As Dr. Conant has remarked, it is an obsolete notion that the generals and admirals do not attach enough importance to science; on the contrary, they are likely to expect too much of it and to support a great deal of work that would be rejected by a conservative foundation officer or industrial executive. And while the scientist or engineer in uniform has moved up to the highest levels in the military staffs, the civilian scientist has become a staff adviser to the Secretary of Defense. The National Security Act of 1947 expected that the Secretary would get his scientific advice from a board made up mainly of representatives of the services. This idea broke down in practice as the Secretary tended to call more and more often on the Chairman of the Research and Development Board for his individual advice. This informal practice, as we have already seen, was made official first by formal order of the Secretary, and later when the Board itself was abolished and its Chairman's position was changed by law to that of an Assistant Secretaryship of Defense. The new Assistant Secretary, with the aid of his staff, is in a position freely to advise the Secretary on any failure of the military planners of take full advantages of the possibilities of research.

But aside from this advice, it is still true that military research and development work is undertaken, with very few exceptions, in accordance with statements of military requirements. Since the O.S.R.D. no civilian agency has been free to develop new ideas for weapons whether the military agencies think they want them or not. And many scientists are still of the opinion that more initiative has been frustrated by military requirements than by any other device ever invented. The remedy sometimes proposed is to set aside a small proportion of the total military development budget to be devoted to a small civilian scientific agency to exploit novel and unconventional ideas. During World War II a small subdivision of the O.S.R.D. known as "Few Quick" was able to turn out a few experimental models of such inventions as the Ground Controlled Approach radar and the Loran navigation system, and to get them rapidly accepted, only because these innovations were controlled by an official who reported only to the President of the United States. Similarly, Dr. Lloyd V. Berkner, the

President of Associated Universities, Inc., has argued that the development of really new weapons and weapons systems, to take full advantage of the opportunities offered by new advances in basic science—new "technological break-throughs" —requires the establishment of a new independent civilian organization very much like the O.S.R.D. of World War II.[2]

With the main purpose of such proposals it is hard to disagree. It is only natural for an existing organization to become stodgy and conservative. The competition among the services does something to prevent this staleness, but not enough. And the Department of Defense would be stronger if it contained a small, flexible, and enterprising experimental organization entirely independent of the military services and reporting directly to the Secretary of Defense.

My question about such a proposal is the difficult question that kept the mice in the fable from adopting a new system of distant early warning: I do not know who is going to bell the cat. The Department of Defense has trouble enough getting the top personnel to fill its staff jobs. Whether it could put together at this time an all-civilian operating organization by recruiting scientists and executives in competition with private industry—private industry which is overburdened with military research contracts—I am far from sure. During the war many of the leading scientists were able to retain their positions in their respective private institutions while working more than a normal full time on government business. In time of peace, when the Attorney General is insisting that all Defense appointees sell their stock in corporations doing business with the military departments, it would be hard to staff a new "Few Quick" or O.S.R.D.-type agency with men of first-

2 Lloyd V. Berkner, "Science and National Strength," an address at the Washington meeting of The American Physical Society, May 1, 1953.

rank ability. And such an agency staffed by second-raters would be worse than none at all.

But the "Few Quick" idea stands as a challenge to the Defense Department. If the Department does not adopt it, it will do well to push in some other directions to broaden the opportunities for initiative and boldness in experimentation—perhaps by giving some of the present institutions with large permanent contracts, such as the Lincoln Laboratory, even more freedom and more adequate resources than they now have to push new types of experimental development.

Another way in which an improvement in organization might set scientists free to make a greater contribution to important policy issues is at the highest level of operations research. While each military service had established programs of operations research during the war, there was no operations research agency to serve the Department of Defense as a whole until 1948. In that year Vannevar Bush persuaded a very dubious Joint Chiefs of Staff to agree to the creation of a Weapons Systems Evaluation Group. The Research and Development Board stood as godparent to this infant; the J.C.S. somewhat grudgingly adopted it.

Now there are a number of reasons why a member of the Joint Chiefs might have been moderately skeptical about the contribution that operations research could make to their work. The J.C.S., by the very nature of their function, have to confine themselves to the broader military problems, usually strategic, and to leave subsidiary details to lower levels in the military services and to commanding officers in the theaters of operations. As the Committee on Operations Research of the National Research Council has pointed out, strategic problems "necessarily involve a large number of subsidiary problems that are not amenable to complete quantitative formulation."[3] By comparison with an operations research agency in one of the military services, therefore, the W.S.E.G. was under a double handicap. It had to work on problems that were broader and more complex and therefore harder to handle by objective scientific research. But, second and more important, it did not work for a single officer who could tell it what subjects to study and what assumptions to make on the aspects of those subjects that were controversial or uncertain. It worked for a committee, the Joint Chiefs of Staff, each of whose members was committed to a somewhat different set of assumptions about military strategy.

Even so, strategy does contain some subsidiary problems that can be solved by the scientific method, to the advantage of the operating official, who then has that many fewer answers to provide by informed guesswork. Operations research cannot give quantitative answers to broad policy questions, but it can still help the official who has to decide to determine the odds. For this reason the J.C.S. might have been expected, while remaining moderately skeptical about the W.S.E.G., to give it a good try. But the fact remains that early this year the professional staff of the W.S.E.G. was only about a dozen in number, while each of the three services had working for it (directly or under contract) operations research staffs numbering hundreds. Moreover, no scientist, after looking over the status and prospects of the W.S.E.G., had been willing to become its Director of Research on a career basis; the two men who had served in that capacity had each been willing to do so only with the safeguard of retaining his permanent university tenure and taking a leave of absence.

The reason was clear enough. If the W.S.E.G. made a study

---

3 Committee on Operations Research, National Research Council, *Operations Research with Special Reference to Non-Military Applications*, April 1951, p. 8.

finding that one weapons system had advantages over another, one military service would be put in danger of losing a part of its "roles and missions" to another. And "roles and missions," it is essential to remember, are to a military service what customers are to a business. Few Chambers of Commerce support Consumers' Research Services.

The Committee on Department of Defense Organization, in early 1953, took a poor view of this situation. It argued that the Secretary of Defense needed the benefit of operations research whether the J.C.S. thought so or not. It recommended that the W.S.E.G. be built up to be at least as strong as the operations research groups of the individual services, and to make this possible it proposed that the Group report to the Secretary not through the J.C.S., but through one of the Assistant Secretaries, who would have no motive for leaving the Group in a comparatively weak status.

Thus in the last few years some important steps have been taken, at least in a tentative and preliminary way, to insure that the Secretary of Defense can get advice and assistance from scientists independent of the normal chain of command. This access is important, and in other Departments as well as Defense, especially since it is essential for the government executive to keep abreast of the changes in society produced by the discoveries of the scientist. I have remarked that most often the controlling questions in government policy are not questions that can be solved by the methods of science. But sometimes they are. Occasionally a new development radically and immediately opens up new possibilities, so that all sorts of national and international policies have to be revised as hurriedly as possible so as to be adapted to it. And always science is producing steady changes in our national life, and the more rapidly we can adapt ourselves to them, or the more effectively we can control them, the better off we shall be.

This leads us to a more difficult question that has been raised by Dr. Lee A. DuBridge, President of California Institute of Technology and Chairman of the Science Advisory Committee of the Office of Defense Mobilization. Dr. DuBridge has argued that "at the very top levels, neither the executive nor the legislative branch has any mechanism for systematically bringing into consideration the scientific and technical aspects of grave national problems."[4]

Specifically, Dr. DuBridge advises that the Chairman of the Atomic Energy Commission should be a regular member of the National Security Council and that the Council should have a Science Advisory Committee with a full-time chairman to advise it on the scientific aspects of its problems.

It seems to me that there are some grave difficulties in this proposal. The first difficulty is a practical one relating to the nature of science. It is the essence of science that no one person can speak for it. On every new practical problem in which science is involved a different scientist is the leading authority. The problem is not to find the single man or the single committee to speak for all science, but to make sure that new voices are heard on each new issue as it arises. The scientific staff work that the President needs, or that the Secretary of Defense needs, is not the work of a laboratory scientist, but of a staff man who can see that all the main channels of scientific advice are kept open—that the opinions of any scientist of stature, provided that they are significant with respect to any major problem, are not prevented from reaching the executive by the prejudices of either bureaucrats and politicians on the one hand or of his fellow scientists on the other.

The second difficulty is political, or almost constitutional. As the history of the Joint Chiefs of Staff shows, it is very easy

4 Lee Alvin DuBridge, "Science and Government," *Chemical and Engineering News*, April 6, 1953, pp. 1384-90.

for an organization to begin with an informal advisory status and gradually acquire something like operating power. It is for this reason that, in the realm of policy advice, it does not always strengthen a position to formalize it and give it authority. It may destroy it entirely. A political executive, if he is to remain effective as an executive, cannot permit anyone in the guise of an adviser to manipulate himself into such a position that the executive cannot freely reject his advice. If the executive permits that, he is well on his way toward the impotent status of a constitutional monarch. The British Prime Minister, having taken over power from the King by just such a procedure, is so well aware of this danger that he makes full use, for his own protection, of the principles of the collective responsibility of the Cabinet and the anonymity of the Civil Service.

If the executive recognizes this principle, his advisers will do well to recognize it too. In the United States the Director of the Budget has become the head of the oldest and most influential staff agency to the President for one all-important reason: in the three decades of the Budget Bureau's history no Congressman or columnist has ever been able to make an important political issue of the fact that the incumbent Director of the Budget had offered advice that the President failed to follow. Budget Directors have given critical and independent advice, but as confidential advisers.

But this is not a role easy for a scientist to accept. His greatest weakness in such a role is his professional conscience, his feeling that he must be the spokesman for his scientific colleagues and for science generally. The Congress has never legislated into existence a position in which a scientist of any description was to be a policy adviser to the President, with a single exception—the Council of Economic Advisers. The story of Dr. Nourse, its first chairman, is the story of a professional economist who tried to protect his dual status as a professional economist and a confidential adviser to the President by refusing to be drawn into public testimony before Congressional committees. But, reading between the lines of his autobiographical account, you can see President Truman growing more and more uncomfortable as he looked over the shoulder of Dr. Nourse at the guiding spirit of the Science of Economics; it must have made him as uneasy as it once made the Queen of Scots to hear the voice of God through the lips of John Knox.

The President cannot be made by institutional arrangements to listen regularly to any specialized advice. One way out is not to listen to the formal adviser. Another is to pay more attention to informal advisers. And another is to appoint to the position of formal adviser a man who is not a specialist. Thus President Truman replaced Dr. Nourse by Leon Keyserling, who was at least as much a lawyer and administrator as an economist. Thus the chairmen of the Atomic Energy Commission, all three of them in turn, have been lawyers and executives rather than nuclear physicists.

The policy staff work around the President would doubtless benefit from a great deal more use of scientific insight and scientific advice. But it would be a mistake, it seems to me, to try to attain this end by providing by law for new members, or for specialized staff advisers, attached to the National Security Council. This is the process of specialism that makes our top policy staff work so weak. On the contrary, we need instead to strengthen the executive generally and to provide him with the discretionary authority and the career staff that he needs in order to bring together all pertinent points of view—certainly including the scientific point of view—before making his decision.

A science itself cannot tell how its own data are to be used.

Its findings cannot be taken undiluted by top political authorities, any more than a scientist's invention can ever be produced by industry just as the scientist invented it. In private industry an invention has first to be developed into a workable product by the engineers; next the production engineers have to make it suitable for mass output by designing it to fit, so far as possible, the machine tool and production facilities already available; and simultaneously it has to be designed so as to fit in with the company's sales program. This is only a pale counterpart of the problem in government, which must decide on the use of any major scientific development in the light of an immense range of policy considerations—social, economic, political, and perhaps military and diplomatic.

This is a problem partly for the engineer and partly for the administrator—both the line administrator who makes decisions more or less on his own and the staff man who shapes up issues for decision by a higher executive. The engineer and the administrator provide an essential layer in the pyramid of government, below the peak of political authority, and above the level at which science must operate.

In application to practical affairs the sciences as such have no common denominator. In a physical sense the engineer provides the common denominator; in a policy sense, the administrator. One of the administrator's tools is the budget, which ought to provide a stable basis for sustained scientific effort and ought to be the means for distributing resources in the most effective way among the various branches of science. It is a poor enough tool in practice, but no one has ever invented a substitute. My former chief, the Chairman of the Research and Development Board, came to that job—even after considerable experience in government—resolved to stick to scientific policy problems and avoid the headaches of the budget. Before his two years in that position had ended, he had found that the budget was his main lever for influencing policy decisions, and that it took up a major share of his time and energy.

The budget, of course, is only one of a number of methods by which the administrator creates a program out of an infinite variety of ill-assorted facts and random possibilities. This is not a feat of individual brilliance, but of group competence; for a group to develop competence, it has to have some continuity and some stability. The reason why civilian scientists are often frustrated in their relation with the military is that the military, with all its faults, does have such continuity and group competence and is not adequately counterbalanced by any corresponding organization or career service on the civilian side of government.

The personnel system of the United States government does not even recognize the need for such an administrative service. Under its rules of civil service classification there is no arrangement for a corps of generalists to deal with the major issues of policy; the administrative officer, indeed, has to justify his existence by making his work into something like a technical specialty or pseudo science. In this respect, of course, government in America simply follows the example of society as a whole, which in business and in education has glorified the specialties and neglected the over-all problem of developing the generalist. When I speak of the administrator and his function I am not thinking of him as he is defined for civil service purposes by the classification experts. That kind of administrator and his function are only an inferior kind of specialty. I am thinking instead of the function described by Brooks Adams:

> Administration is the capacity of co-ordinating many, and often conflicting, social energies in a single organism, so adroitly that they shall operate as a unity. . . . Probably no very highly

specialized class can be strong in this intellectual quality because of the intellectual isolation incident to specialization; and yet administration or generalization is not only the faculty upon which social stability rests, but is, possibly, the highest faculty of the human mind.[5]

Many scientists, especially those from universities, never feel the need for such a function. The purpose of organization and administration in a university is mainly to care for the material needs of a collection of independent disciplines. There have been some ambitious efforts to bring them together in the name of general education, but the going has been rough. On the other hand, in public affairs (including the great foundations as well as government) the administrator is not motivated by a merely philosophical purpose: he sees the need for stamping out hookworm or the boll weevil; he sees the need for an improved system of communications; he sees the need for an effective system of air defense. And it is his job to marshal the forces of science into an effective program and to keep them from going off into the entirely different directions of their several disciplines and specialties. Unless this essential job of the administrator is done, the whole program of government will not become coherent enough to be controlled by the political authorities who in turn are responsible to the people.

But if science, as such, cannot give us automatic answers to our great issues of public policy, that does not mean that scientists cannot play an important role in answering them. The administrator and the scientist are not two quite different categories of people. Indeed, it seems to me that the whole history of American government shows that the scientist and the engineer have often moved successfully into many of the most responsible and difficult administrative positions. In this

[5] Brooks Adams, *The Theory of Social Revolutions* (New York: The Macmillan Company, 1913), pp. 207-8.

respect American government has had an experience similar to that of American private business.

On the aspects of administration that are managerial in the narrow sense of the word, the scientist whose only experience has been the laboratory is often poorly prepared. Moreover, he is likely to dismiss as unimportant those aspects of an administrative job that have to do with keeping the organization and procedures in good repair and keeping the majority of the staff satisfied with their work. The reason may be that he is tempted by force of mental habit to concentrate on those aspects of his job that are most interesting to the individual student as intellectual problems—a temptation which the administrator usually cannot afford to yield to.

These considerations argue, it seems to me, for having a few men with quite general administrative background in the top ranks of even those agencies with heavily scientific programs. On the other hand, I would argue with equal emphasis that the administrative personnel of almost all agencies ought to have a fair proportion of men with some training and experience in science and engineering. If administration is to serve as a useful layer in the pyramid of policy between the peak of political power and the base of science and technology, it needs in its composition an appropriate mixture of general competence and special knowledge.

Many policy problems that cannot be solved precisely by scientific research can in practice be solved satisfactorily only by men with scientific knowledge as well as administrative ability. In military affairs, for example, there are many issues on which it is not practical to look to operations research for the answers, but which cannot be handled properly without the kind of judgment that comes from scientific background. The Canadian government recognized this principle when it made its leading civilian scientist a member of its equivalent of the Joint Chiefs of Staff. The scientist should take part as a responsible administrator, right up to the highest levels, in making decisions that cannot be based entirely on objective research, and on which no irresponsible adviser can ever expect to be consulted.

In the administrative corps some mixture of general and special qualifications is desirable. In the long run, however, a mere mixture of unrelated skills is not what is needed. What is needed is a corps of men whose liberal education includes an appreciation of the role of science and technology in society and whose scientific education has not been a narrowly technical or vocational one, but has treated science as one of the highest intellectual endeavors of men who also have responsibility as free citizens. The humanities and the social sciences are too often taught in America as narrowly technical subjects. We can hardly found a new generation of administrative generalists on them as they are commonly taught today.

It will not do to adopt as our ultimate ideal the pattern of a completely separate administrative class, set up in an administrative career that is a lifetime business and virtually closed to men whose experience in their twenties and thirties has been in science or technology. This is the pattern of the Administrative Class of the British civil service, which has been based traditionally on the recruitment of men trained primarily in the humanities, history, and politics as taught at the two pre-eminent English universities. That career corps richly deserves the praise that it has long received as a keystone of integrity and efficiency for the government of the United Kingdom.

The British Administrative Class is a great deal more efficient than its chaotic counterpart in the United States government. It is probably a great deal better than anything we shall ever get if we do no better than we have been doing lately.

But I do not think that our main possibility of improvement lies in an effort to imitate it.

Any such closed service is a profoundly conservative force—not in the sense of being opposed to left-wing economics (as British Socialists used to charge, in the days before they came to power), but in the sense of looking on the government and its program as a single coherent machine in which inconsistencies cannot be permitted. Any novel idea is an inconsistency that could cause temporary waste and disorder and inefficiency and would probably detract from the current program.

As much as I should like to see a more satisfactory administrative service in the United States government, offering a much more attractive permanent career to a larger proportion of its officials, it seems to me that there is a great deal of merit in continuing to have many of its members drawn from earlier experience in the professional and scientific specialties, in private as well as public life. With all the disadvantages of the American public service as it now exists, we can see even now some advantages in basing our system of administrative careers on such a mixed foundation. The professional ties that the government administrators retain with their professional colleagues outside the government keep them from considering current issues solely from the point of view either of the party in power or of the convenience of the governmental organization. Those same ties help to keep them alert to new ideas and willing to support a certain number of varying and independent programs. Their variety of experience gives them more sympathy with the functions and the point of view of the private and local institution, and it helps to keep the federal system and the system of contractual relationships truly decentralized, varied, and more likely to retain the vigor and initiative that characterize a free society.

It would be comforting to hope that in the long run the

development of science, especially of the social sciences, will let us solve all human problems by the scientific method. But this is not a prospect that seems possible in theory, to say nothing of its being likely in practice.

We need not hang onto this hope in order to further the development of science. For there are plenty of worlds for the scientist to conquer. And he may have an even better chance to get on with his job if all of us realize that the major policy decisions on which society depends must be made only partly on the basis of the exact quantitative data that scientific research can provide. For then we can all understand the necessity of creating the kind of responsible political and administrative systems within which free science will have its fullest opportunity for public service.

VII

NEW WINE
IN NEW BOTTLES

Those who believe in free government and free science have
been discouraged, in the mid-twentieth century, by two unpleas-
ant facts. One is that the apparently steady advance of the
nineteenth century toward democratic and responsible government has been arrested by the rise of dictatorships and the
spread of a philosophy of tyranny. The other is that mankind
has discovered means by which military aggression, using atomic power, could certainly destroy civilization as we know it,
if not indeed all life on the planet.[1]

These two facts have forced the United States to pour money
into research programs for new weapons. As science becomes
an active ally of military power we shall do well to understand
the principles that have guided its relation to government in
America. For the influence of science has been the source of
some of the most vital elements in the American system of
government, and the same influence does much to explain a
few of its faults as well as many of its virtues. An understanding
of this influence may even help us persuade some other parts
of the world that democracy in America has some dynamic
qualities that in the future can both strengthen its force and
safeguard its freedom.

[1] "Physical scientists have now found means which, if they are developed,
can wipe life off the surface of this planet. Those words that I speak are
words that can be taken literally." Speech by Secretary of State John Foster
Dulles before the United Nations General Assembly, September 17, 1953.

But however hopeful we may be, we have to face the unhappy facts that democracy has been put on the defensive in many parts of the world and that new weapons of destruction are a constant threat to free civilization. These two facts are forcing us to reconsider some ideas that were firm articles of faith in the days of our fathers and grandfathers. Following the American and French revolutions, liberal thinkers were inclined to believe that, since man was fundamentally good, he needed only to remove the artificial constraints of government in order to reach an ultimate state of perfection. This general idea was, paradoxically enough, at the root of the philosophy of the laissez-faire economists and of their most extreme opponents, the Marxists, who thought that men would have no more political troubles when the state had withered away.

About the same time that the popular thought of the Western world (and especially the United States) believed in the automatic progress of mankind toward democracy, scientists were inclined to believe in a neat mechanical system of cause and effect, comprehending everything from the fundamental laws of mathematics and physics to the motives and morals of men. Accordingly, many came to hope that the gradual extension of scientific knowledge would be the motive power for an infinite progress in politics and economics. And just as politicians and economists believed that political progress would depend on a reduction in the powers of government, so the scientists were sure that the advancement of knowledge would be guaranteed if science and scientific institutions could be protected from the interference of politicians.

This coincidence of political and scientific thought—more profound scholars than I will have to say which type of thinking had the greater influence over the other—was the basis of the self-confidence of the Western intellectual world a half century ago. Neither idea is quite so firmly held today. Political theorists have yielded their easy optimism to the logic of facts that every newspaper reader understands, and the philosophers of science have been driven by the new developments in mathematical physics to accept the possibility that science may never possess the key to an understanding of the ultimate structure of nature.

As some people became disillusioned about the possibilities of the infinite extension of knowledge and the infinite perfectibility of mankind, they looked for another absolute faith. Some turned to the new dogma of Communism, which promised to make politics over with the aid of a scientific dialectic. The more intelligent among them have long since learned better, with the benefit of the Soviet Union's demonstration of the practical workings of Communism. Others came to believe quite systematically that our present difficulties come from having taken up science and technology too enthusiastically; they can see a way out of our difficulties only in a return to some authoritative philosophical system and in the establishment of a governing elite to rule according to its principles. They think, in short, that the hunger for experimental knowledge was the sin that put man into the cruel difficulties of the modern world, and they wish to reverse the process by restoring traditional systems of belief and the institutions that they supported.

But I see no hope in trying to get back into the Garden of Eden. That way there is no salvation. We have to accept, as individuals and as members of a political system, the responsibilities that new knowledge brings to us. If the Western world is to resist the spread of tyranny and its theories, perhaps we need most of all a clearer faith or philosophy on which to build the institutions of free government and free science— or a clearer understanding of the one we already have. Some may try to supply this faith, after the fashion of philosophers, by abstract reason. Others among us may take a more modest approach and try first to understand (and then to improve) the ways in which our institutions are presently constituted—ways that many of our people, and perhaps even a few of our philosophers, may not be aware of. As we do so we are likely to find that science has had a profound effect from the very beginning on the nature of the American political system, partly through the direct application of research and partly through the general climate of informed opinion and the influence of professional groups that have scientific backgrounds and interests. And the American government has consequently developed in ways particularly congenial to the application of science to public affairs. With science as important as it is likely to be in the future of society, these aspects of American government may yet become great assets.

Revolutions are perhaps successful less often because the revolutionists are powerful or cunning than because the old institutions have decayed too much to withstand the new pressures. Men all too often put new wine into old bottles, with unhappy results. Thus the revolutions of the eighteenth and the nineteenth centuries that brought new republics into existence did not all create constitutional systems stable enough for the twentieth century. All of them struck down the authority of the hereditary sovereign and increased the control of the legislature over the chief executive. But some of these republics collapsed because, while they maintained these principles, they failed to take note of new threats. The eighteenth-century principles held good as defenses against the dynasties, but not against the dictatorships. The fanatical and doctrinaire party, the concentration of economic power, and the monolithic bureaucracy put into power dictators some of whom never needed to assume a formal position of executive responsibility. But against each of these three threats the United States has been given some protection by the way in which science has helped to build her governmental institutions.

Of the three great threats to twentieth-century democracy, the most dangerous has been the doctrinaire party. The greatest danger to the freedom of Western Europe today is that a powerful minority of the people, including many of the intellectual leaders, have lost their sense of loyalty to their nation as a whole and have transferred that loyalty to some party doctrine or to one totalitarian ideology or another. The loyalty to party above nation has made governments weak and unstable and has made it hard to develop a steady consensus or moderate policy.

The United States has escaped this fate, partly no doubt, because she has shared some of the legal and political traditions that have given the English-speaking nations an unusual ability to reconcile freedom with responsible authority. But this explanation is only part of the story. For the United States does not by any means share all of the legal and political traditions of the rest of the English-speaking world. Indeed, she was the first large Western nation to repudiate the keystone of that tradition—the belief in a hereditary monarchy as the unifying force in a political system and as the constitutional basis of the authority of government and of the loyalty of His Majesty's subjects.

By contrast the citizen of the American republic has no such political anchor. In the eighteenth century he joined the scientists and rationalists (and the religious dissenters) in believing that the myth of hereditary rule was a superstition that supported political oppression, and he followed with enthusiasm the efforts of the lawyers to construct on republican principles constitutions in which the people alone should be sovereign. Today Americans have generally lost their aversion to the British monarchy; some, indeed, look on it rather wistfully as a stabilizing influence that we are the poorer for having given up. But we cannot create again, by any artificial process, a belief in an institution that we once led the world in rejecting. Our strength will lie, instead, in understanding the merits of our own executive and in improving it by means the most consistent with our own habits and traditions.

Under the sovereign people, the American Presidency has been the main protection of the Constitution against the doctrinaire party. The Presidency has given the United States what most of the nations that tried to graft the British parliamentary system onto republican constitutions do not have: an executive accountable to both an independent legislature and an independent judiciary, but nevertheless strong enough to protect itself against irresponsible or fanatical factions.

And there is an even more important safeguard. For the Presidency itself could easily be weakened if it were not supported by the general consensus of the nation. That consensus cannot be based—as at bottom the loyalty of the British to their King is based—on a traditional, indeed almost mystical, allegiance. It must rest on a belief in the law (especially the Constitution) and in an objective if not a scientific approach to the facts.

The Declaration of Independence appealed from the authority of the sovereign to the laws of Nature and of Nature's God. And ever since, the lawyer and the scientist have had a role in the American public service quite unlike their role in the United Kingdom or most other democratic states. The unusual role of the lawyer in American public life has been recognized ever since Burke took note of it in his famous speech on conciliation with America. But the scientist, too, moved into the gap that was left by the abolition of the Crown and of the ruling class and the career public service that clustered about that fountain of honors. The authority and the competence of government were so weakened in the United States in the early nineteenth century that it was quite unable to meet its modern responsibilities. And science played a notable role in building up the powers and functions of government and in shaping its administrative institutions. The American system of government has been called one of permanent revolution; it would be even more to the point, it seems to me, to consider it a continuous Constitutional convention—a process of continuous revision of our governing institutions, with the processes of research and organizations of scientists playing more of a role than is generally recognized.

American patriotism and loyalty, by contrast with British patriotism and loyalty, depend far less on devotion to the person of the Chief of State and far less on the sentiment and the historical tradition associated with rank and with ceremony. It is made up rather more heavily of faith in our Constitutional system—a faith qualified by the idea that, as James Kent expressed it in 1794, "the goodness of these institutions will brighten on free investigation and faithful experiment."[2]

The consensus that sustains the unity of the United States could readily be destroyed if most people believed that the government's policies and organization should be developed in accord with their partisan ideologies rather than in accord with the facts as shown by research and experimentation. It is the attitude of willingness to adjust one's partisan views to the facts (rather than vice versa) that enables the Presidency to produce something like an integrated national program.

This attitude is built into the nature of our institutions. It accounts for the almost nonpartisan approach to policy issues of the better Congressional committees and for the close rela-

[2] From a lecture by James Kent at Columbia College in 1794, quoted by Chief Justice Earl Warren in a speech at the Columbia Bicentennial, January 14, 1954.

tions of specialists in the federal government with their professional colleagues in state and local government or in private life. Then, too, it sometimes accounts for stubborn and irresponsible stalemates, since every man can hire his own lawyer and his own expert, and for the lack of responsibility in our political parties, which feel little obligation to support a coherent and workable program, even when it is presented by their own leaders.

As a result the new policies of government—the new functions and powers adopted—have not usually been decided on the basis of party platforms. Instead, they have often followed the initiative of scientific and professional groups in both the government and private life—groups that have sought means of dealing with the difficult problems involved in the development of the new continent, in the industrialization of our cities, and in the assumption of world leadership. And the most effective criticism of government policies in the most difficult fields often comes, not from party leaders, but from scientific and professional groups that are able—or at least comparatively able—to think in terms of the national rather than a partisan interest.

A second threat to free institutions, and one that has been a particular concern of the scientist, is the danger that comes from a concentration of economic power. This danger is, of course, a general one; if economic power is completely centralized, a great centralization of political authority must necessarily follow. But the danger applies particularly to science. For the modern necessity of using science for military purposes makes it impossible to dream any longer of protecting science by setting it aside in institutions completely independent of the federal government. As a matter of fact, the new financial structure of society, including the progressive income tax, made this impossible even before we were so clearly faced with the problem of protecting ourselves against both domestic sub-version and the long-range bomber or guided missile.

As we seek to develop our government's organization for the support of science and its application to practical problems, one of our difficulties is the great difference between the approach of the scientist and that of the average citizen—or between the approach of the scientist and that of the politician and administrator who share and represent the attitudes of the average citizen. For the scientist and the average citizen are always likely to think in different ways about problems of administration, public or private. The scientist is devoted to the search for truth; to make this search possible, he needs the support and protection of institutions independent of the fluctuations and pressures of business competition or of politics. The average citizen, on the other hand, is not much interested in abstract truth; he wants what science can give him. Accordingly, with all the weight of his vote and his purchasing power, he presses science to gear itself to the production of new material advantages—new ways of feeding and clothing the people, new comforts, new playthings, new cures, new weapons.

This disparity leads, at worst, to an unhappy deadlock: the politician and the administrator want a system in which they can direct science to practical ends by control of the purse strings, and the scientist wants one that will give him support without sacrificing his independence. This is an overstatement of the contrast, for few on either side are so dogmatic as not to adjust their views a little in the direction of the other. But something like this difference of attitude has been involved in the principal disputes over the government's policy for the support of science and over the nature of its administrative machinery for that purpose.

It is easy to exaggerate this difference of opinion. The historian of government and of science can make a great deal of the quarrels over the basic legislation that set the pattern for the government's support of science after World War II. But the differences of opinion were less significant than the shifts that brought men together. The most striking single fact about the role of science in public affairs after World War II was that the leaders of both sides of the argument had come to an agreement on essentials that neither would have considered possible a decade earlier. The leading scientists of the country came to advocate the creation of permanent governmental machinery for the direct support of science, and especially for strengthening its relation with military affairs, while it became the official policy of the Administration, even with the concurrence of the Director of the Budget, to commit the government to the expenditure of large funds for research in private institutions.

As this machinery was constructed and these funds were spent, the striking fact was that the private institutions that took part in the program retained their independence and became strong partners in a new relationship that almost amounted to an improvised system of federalism. Their independence was certainly not complete; like state and local governments, research institutions became able to assert only a relative degree of autonomy in society. But that degree of independence was great enough to make them strong and aggressive critics of federal policy as well as enterprising agents of its execution.

The economic system of the nation has become thoroughly interdependent, and the fiscal influence of the federal government penetrates all segments of our society. But, particularly in those fields that involve the most advanced scientific work, we have experimented with patterns of organization and financing that can effectively decentralize even those operations in which the interest of the national government is most clearly paramount. As a result we have a workable alternative to socialism. We simply do not have to accept the dilemma between the anarchist and the socialist, for we have learned various ways of giving to the central government a certain amount of general influence or control over the economy without destroying the freedom and independence of private institutions.

Finally, the nation has developed its public service in such a way as to avoid creating a closed bureaucracy. It has given the scientist in private life a considerable opportunity to help determine public policy and to assist in its execution through an elaborate system of advisory machinery. Moreover, it has kept the channels of appointment and promotion in the regular civil service open to the scientist and the engineer, not only for specialized positions, but up to the highest nonpolitical positions in the Administration. The government personnel system, indeed, has been founded on the scientific specialties. It was on the basis of their professional standards that the civil service system, in its higher ranks, was first freed from partisan patronage, as the government took over functions too complex for the party hack to handle. And the federal government is free to bring into its top nonpolitical positions the most com- petent men that it can find, from private as well as public careers.

Thus science has helped to bring up to date the ideas of democracy that were developed in America during the early years of the republican revolution, and to give them a new meaning suited to an age of technology. We no longer believe that government must restrict its functions to the minimum that the Jeffersonians thought possible, but we do hope to see its policies formulated and administered on an objective basis, and to see private institutions take part in this process and carry on research on the policies of the government and the nature of its machinery. We no longer expect our local institutions—universities as well as state and local governments—to remain entirely independent of the federal government in their financing, but we want the administrative relationship so organized as to protect their independence, both in their own operations and in their criticism of central authority. We no longer believe with the Jacksonians in the spoils system and rotation in office, but we like to see the top administrative structure of the government receive frequent infusions of men with new ideas, including many with scientific and technical backgrounds and with extended experience in private occupations. These principles may yet help us establish institutions of government fit to deal with the problems of the atomic age—new bottles capable of containing the new wine of the late twentieth century, for all its powerful ferment.

These are assets, or at least potential assets, in dealing with the problems of the future. But we must admit that we do not yet know how to manage our assets very well. In particular, we have a grave weakness at the very center of our governmental machinery. We do not have an adequate career system for the higher ranks of administrators in the federal government.

For this reason there is a dangerous element of irresponsibility built into the central structure of the executive branch. The various specialized units of the executive departments charge ahead, each in its own way, with tremendous energy, impelled by the administrative and political drive of the private interests the most directly concerned with their programs. High above them the President and his political family do their best to find out what they are doing, to guide and control them, and to be responsible to the people and to the Congress for their policies and their administration. But the job of the political executive is impossible unless it is supported by an organized system of professional administration. For the lack of such a system the control of responsible political executives over the whole governmental machine is often little more than a constitutional fiction, and the control of the Congress is even less effective. We have a high-speed machine, but we do not know where we are going.

The weakness of this administrative layer creates another dangerous defect in our system of government. It forces the research scientist and the specialist to assume responsibilities semipolitical in nature, simply because no one else is available to assume them. The consequence is often that the research scientist or specialist comes under political attack and is driven out of the public service. Or, if he is a part-time adviser or consultant, he is tempted into public debate over issues that can be effectively discussed only among professionals. The weakness of general administration in American government does not create new opportunities for scientists: it makes it impossible to develop a clear understanding of their role or to provide terms of service that will be attractive to the most competent among them.

You may well ask whether it is not inconsistent to argue for a more adequate administrative career service just after arguing that the administrative service ought not to be a closed corps and that it ought to include a considerable proportion of men with background in science and with experience in private life. I think that this is not at all inconsistent. On the contrary, it seems to me that the only hope for an adequate administrative corps in the American government is to build it in part on the generalist with a background in general management and general public affairs, and in part on the man who has become a generalist after a thorough grounding in one of the specialized sciences or in its engineering or managerial application.

But an administrative system is only a reflection of the hopes and beliefs and skills of individual human beings. The top administrative service of the nation cannot exist without the support of informed public opinion or without the participation of men whose appreciation of public affairs is broader than that of any specialty. Here, then, is the opportunity for the American university—to educate in the humanities and the social sciences men who have an understanding of the role of the natural sciences in government and society, and to educate natural scientists who can appreciate the problems faced by the politician and the administrator, and who will, some of them, shoulder the burdens of the direct administration of national affairs.

The skeptical and questioning approach of science has played a major part in freeing the United States from the authority of old tradition and protecting her from the fanaticism of new ideologies. The restless energy of the scientist and the engineer has broken through the constraints of red tape and supplied a dynamic drive to the development of government programs, as well as to the productiveness of private industry. But the problems that the United States faces today cannot all be solved by rebellious independence and restless energy. The role of world leadership is an uncomfortable one; it requires a steadiness of purpose, an economy in the use of our energies, and a breadth of philosophy that have never been characteristic of the American temper. We may well pray that we shall be given time to develop them.

GALAXY BOOKS

Aaron, Daniel   *Men of Good Hope*   GB58

Abrams, Meyer H., ed.   *English Romantic Poets*   GB35

Agarwala and Singh, eds.   *The Economics of Underdevelopment*   GB97

Ashton, T. S.   *The Industrial Revolution*   GB109

Austin, J. L.   *How To Do Things with Words*   GB132

Sense and Sensibilia   GB108

Barker, Ernest, ed. & tr.   *The Politics of Aristotle*   GB69

ed.   *Social Contract:*
Essays by Locke, Hume, Rousseau   GB68

Bate, Walter Jackson   *The Achievement of Samuel Johnson*   GB53

Berlin, Isaiah   *Karl Marx: His Life and Environment*   GB25

Bogard and Oliver, eds.   *Modern Drama*   GB138

Bowle, John   *Politics and Opinion in the 19th Century*   GB119

Bowra, C. M.   *Ancient Greek Literature*   GB30

The Romantic Imagination   GB54

Bridenbaugh, Carl and Jessica   *Rebels and Gentlemen:*
Philadelphia in the Age
of Franklin   GB141

Brower, Reuben A.   *The Fields of Light*   GB87

Bruun, Geoffrey   *Nineteenth Century European Civilization*   GB36

Bush, Douglas   *English Poetry*   GB93

Clark, George   *Early Modern Europe*   GB37

The Seventeenth Century   GB47

Clifford, James L.   *Biography as an Art*   GB70

ed.   *Eighteenth-Century English Literature*   GB23

Cochrane, Charles Norris   *Christianity and Classical Culture*   GB7

Collingwood, R. G.   *The Idea of History*   GB1

The Idea of Nature   GB31

The Principles of Art   GB11

Cragg, Kenneth   *The Call of the Minaret*   GB122

Craig, Gordon A.   *The Politics of the Prussian Army, 1640-1945*   GB118

Cruickshank, John   *Albert Camus and the Literature of Revolt*   GB43

Davis, Herbert   *Jonathan Swift: Essays on His Satire*
and Other Studies   GB106

Dean, Leonard, ed.   *Shakespeare*   GB46

Dixon, W. MacNeile   *The Human Situation*   GB12

Ellmann, Richard   *The Identity of Yeats*   GB126

Feidelson and Brodtkorb, eds.   *Interpretation of American Literature*   GB26

Frankel, Joseph   *International Relations*   GB117

Gerould, Gordon Hall   *The Ballad of Tradition*   GB8

Gerth, H. H., and Mills, C. Wright, eds. & trs.   *From Max Weber:*
Essays in Sociology   GB13

Gibb, H. A. R.   *Mohammedanism*   GB90

Gilby, Thomas, ed. & tr.   *St. Thomas Aquinas: Philosophical Texts*   GB29

Grierson, Herbert, ed.   *Metaphysical Lyrics
                                and Poems of the Seventeenth Century*   GB19
Halsband, Robert   *The Life of Lady Mary Wortley Montagu*   GB44
Hare, R. M.   *Freedom and Reason*   GB134
                    The Language of Morals   GB111
Heiler, Friedrich   *Prayer*,   translated by Samuel McComb   GB16
Heimann, Eduard   *History of Economic Doctrines*   GB123
Highet, Gilbert   *The Classical Tradition*   GB5
                    Juvenal the Satirist   GB48
Hobhouse, L. T.   *Liberalism*   GB120
Hoffman, Daniel   *Form and.Fable in American Fiction*   GB137
Kaplan, Abraham   *American Ethics and Public Policy*   GB99
Kaufmann, R. J., ed.   *Elizabethan Drama*   GB63
Keast, William R., ed.   *Seventeenth-Century English Poetry*   GB89
Kennedy, Charles, ed. & tr.   *Early English Christian Poetry*   GB94
Kerr, C., Dunlop, J. T., Harbison, F. H., & Myers, C. A.
                    Industrialism and Industrial Man   GB107
Kitto, H. D. F., tr.   *Sophocles: Three Tragedies:
                                Antigone; Oedipus the King; Electra*   GB114
Kline, Morris   *Mathematics in Western Culture*   GB128
Koch, Adrienne   *Jefferson and Madison: The Great Collaboration*   GB110
Knox, Ronald A.   *Enthusiasm*   GB59
Langer, Susanne K., ed.   *Reflections on Art*   GB60
Lewis, C. S.   *The Allegory of Love*   GB17
                    A Preface to Paradise Lost   GB57
Lindsay, A. D.   *The Modern Democratic State*   GB86
Litz, A. Walton   *The Art of James Joyce*   GB121
            ed.   *Modern American Fiction*   GB100
Lowrie, Walter, tr.   *Kierkegaard: Christian Discourses*   GB49
Livingstone, Richard, ed. & tr.   *Thucydides:
                                The History of the Peloponnesian War*   GB33
MacNeice, Louis, tr.   *Goethe's Faust*   GB45
Malinowski, Bronislaw   *A Scientific Theory of Culture*   GB40
Matthiessen, F. O.   *The Achievement of T. S. Eliot*   GB22
                    Henry James. The Major Phase   GB103
Matthiessen, F. O., and Murdock, Kenneth B., eds.   *The Notebooks
                                    of Henry James*   GB61
Mills, C. Wright   *The Power Elite*   GB20
                    White Collar   GB3
Montagu, Ashley, ed.   *Culture and the Evolution of Man*   GB88
Morison, Samuel Eliot   *Sources and Documents Illustrating
                            the American Revolution, 1764-1788,
                            and the Formation of the Federal
                            Constitution*   GB135
Moss, H. St. L. B.   *The Birth of the Middle Ages, 395-814*   GB130
Muller, Herbert J.   *The Uses of the Past*   GB9
Mure, G. R. G.   *Aristotle*   GB113

Murray, Gilbert	*The Rise of the Greek Epic*	GB41
Nicholas, H. G.	*The United Nations as a Political Institution*	GB105
Nicolson, Harold	*Diplomacy*	GB115
Nisbet, Robert A.	*Community and Power*	GB91
Otto, Rudolf	*The Idea of the Holy*	GB14
Peterson, Merrill D.	*The Jefferson Image in the American Mind*	GB71
Price, Don K.	*Government and Science*	GB72
Radhakrishnan, S.	*Eastern Religions and Western Thought*	GB27
Richards, I. A.	*The Philosophy of Rhetoric*	GB131
Roberts, David E.	*Existentialism and Religious Belief,* edited by Roger Hazelton	GB28
Rosenthal, M. L.	*The Modern Poets: A Critical Introduction*	GB139
Rostovtzeff, M.	*Greece*	GB98
	Rome	GB42
Russell, Bertrand	*The Problems of Philosophy*	GB21
	Religion and Science	GB50
Schelling, Thomas C.	*The Strategy of Conflict*	GB101
Schorer, Mark, ed.	*Modern British Fiction*	GB64
Schumpeter, Joseph A.	*Ten Great Economists: From Marx to Keynes*	GB140
	The Theory of Economic Development, translated by Redvers Opie	GB55
Sesonske, Alexander	*Value and Obligation: The Foundations of an Empiricist Ethical Theory*	GB125
Shapiro, Harry L., ed.	*Man, Culture, and Society*	GB32
Shaw, T. E., tr.	*The Odyssey of Homer*	GB2
Sinclair, John D., ed.& tr.	*Dante's Inferno*	GB65
	Dante's Purgatorio	GB66
	Dante's Paradiso	GB67
Slonim, Marc	*The Epic of Russian Literature:* *From Its Origins through Tolstoy*	GB127
	From Chekhov to the Revolution	GB92
Tarski, Alfred	*Introduction to Logic and to the Methodology of Deductive Sciences*	GB133
Thomson, David	*World History: 1914-1961*	GB116
Thomson, George	*The Atom*	GB95
Tillich, Paul	*Love, Power and Justice*	GB38
	Theology of Culture	GB124
Toynbee, Arnold J.	*A Study of History, Volume 1*	GB74
	A Study of History, Volume 2	GB75
	A Study of History, Volume 3	GB76
	A Study of History, Volume 4	GB77
	A Study of History, Volume 5	GB78
	A Study of History, Volume 6	GB79
	A Study of History, Volume 7A	GB80
	A Study of History, Volume 7B	GB81
	A Study of History, Volume 8	GB82

	A Study of History, Volume 9	GB83
	A Study of History, Volume 10	GB84
	A Study of History, Volume 12	GB85
Turberville, A. S.	English Men and Manners in the Eighteenth Century	GB10
Wagenknecht, Edward, ed.	Chaucer	GB24
Ward, John William	Andrew Jackson: Symbol for an Age	GB73
Wedgwood, C. V.	Seventeenth-Century English Literature	GB51
Wheare, K. C.	Federal Government	GB112
	Legislatures	GB104
Whitehead, Alfred North	An Introduction to Mathematics	GB18
Wilson, Edmund	The Triple Thinkers	GB96
	The Wound and the Bow: Seven Studies in Literature	GB136
Woodward, C. Vann	Tom Watson: Agrarian Rebel	GB102
	The Strange Career of Jim Crow	GB6
Wright, Austin, ed.	Victorian Literature	GB52
Young, G. M.	Victorian England: Portrait of an Age	GB129
Young, J. Z.	Doubt and Certainty in Science	GB34
Zaehner, R. C.	Mysticism Sacred and Profane	GB56
Zimmern, Alfred	The Greek Commonwealth	GB62

HESPERIDES BOOKS

Clifford, James	Young Sam Johnson	HS5
Einstein, Alfred	Mozart: His Character, His Work	HS8
Falls, Cyril	The Art of War from the Age of Napoleon to the Present Day	HS3
Ferguson, George	Signs and Symbols in Christian Art	HS1
Fry, Christopher	Three Plays: The Firstborn; Thor, with Angels; A Sleep of Prisoners	HS4
Ibsen, Henrik	An Enemy of the People; The Wild Duck; Rosmersholm	HS2
Tolstoy, Leo	What is Art? and Essays on Art	HS6